THE PROTAGONISTS

BY PICA WU

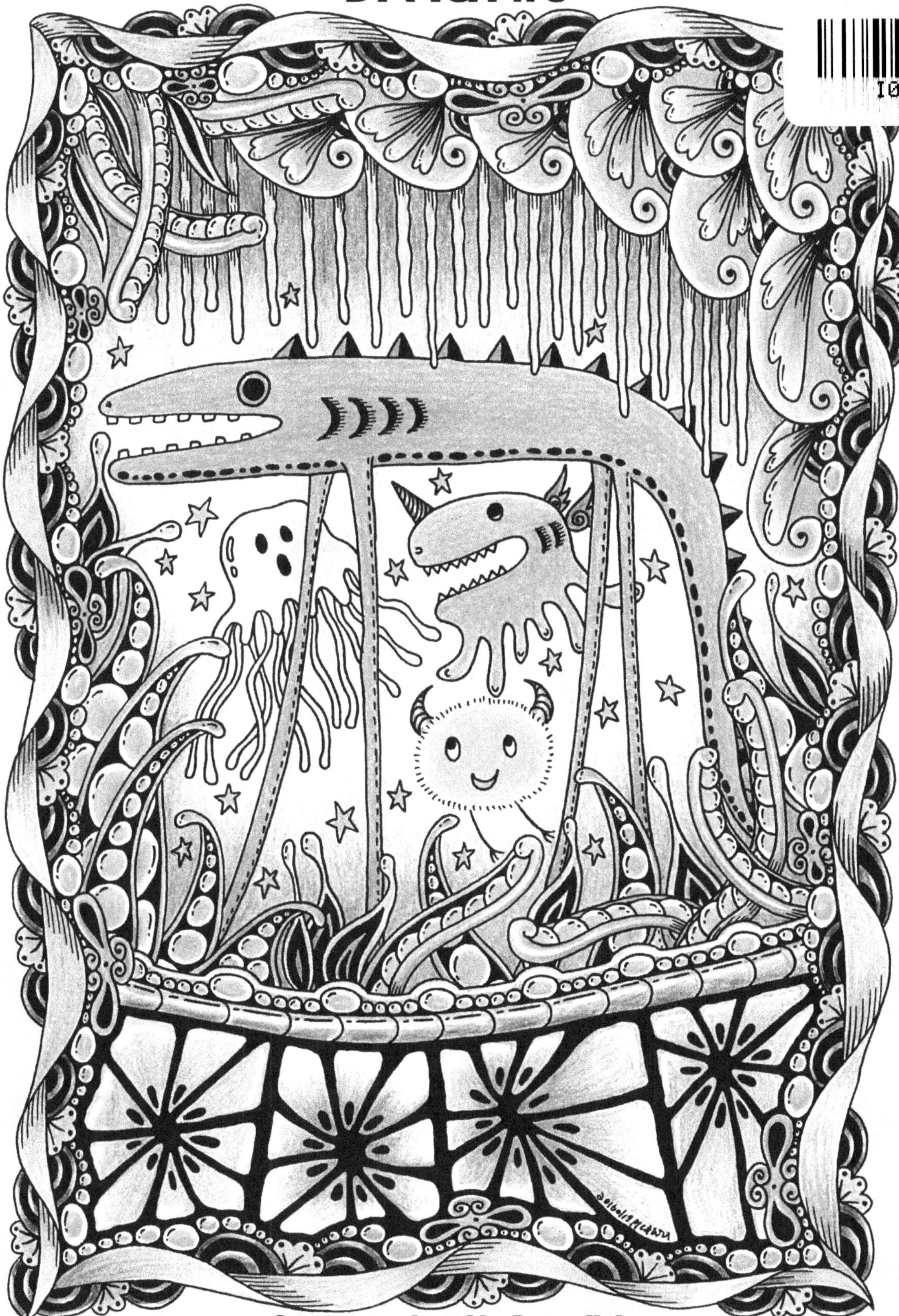

Coverart colored by Rover Hsiao

Published by
"GDG©"
Global Doodle Gems

Share your colored versions with us ! We love seeing your results and hearing from you
we are social !

The Official FB book page, stay on top of what we have in the works !
www.facebook.com/globaldoodlegems
The Community group, share your colored pages, meet the artists, enjoy exclusive freebies, take part in community Charity books and so much more......
www.facebook.com/groups/globaldoodlegems/
Follow us on Twitter.... @GlobalDoodlegem
We are on Instagram too
@globaldoodlegems for instagram
...and if you are not social like that we have a blog
globaldoodlegems.wordpress.com

All of us from the Global Doodle Gems wish you a colortastic time and look forward to seeing your wonderful color results online !

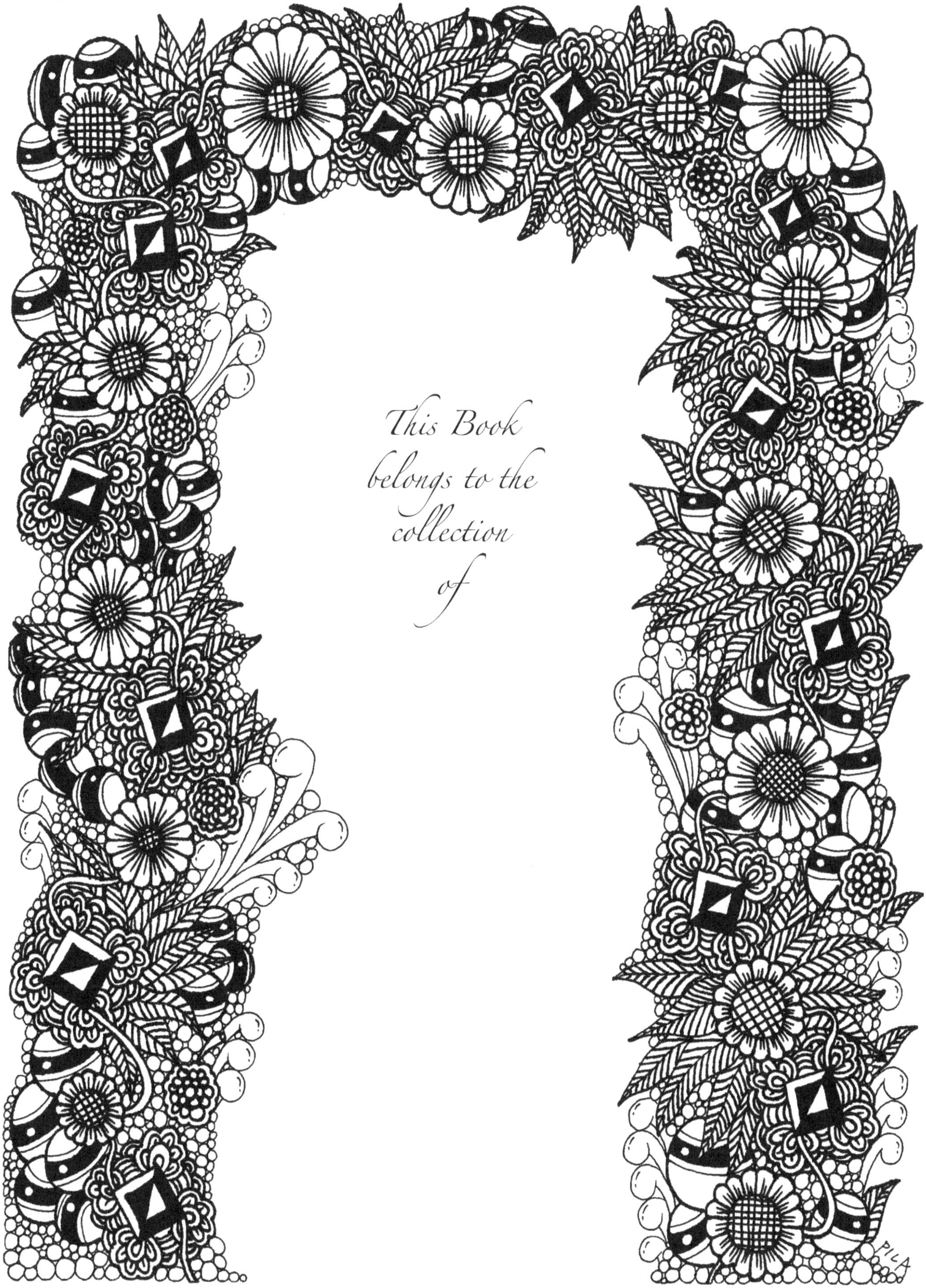

This Book
belongs to the
collection
of

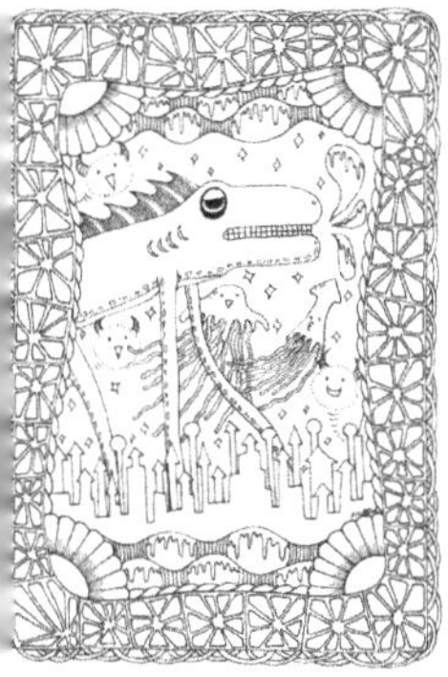
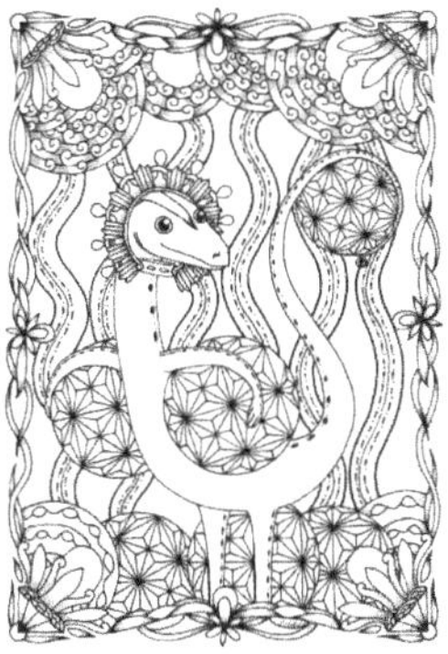
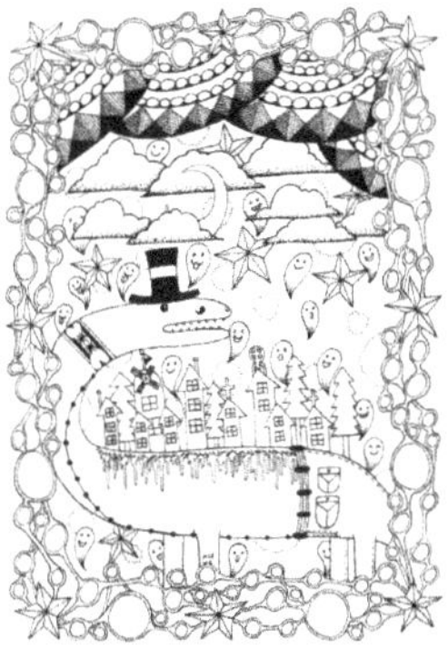
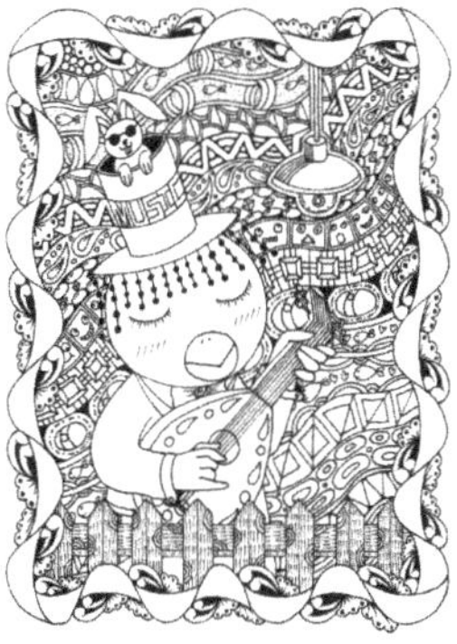
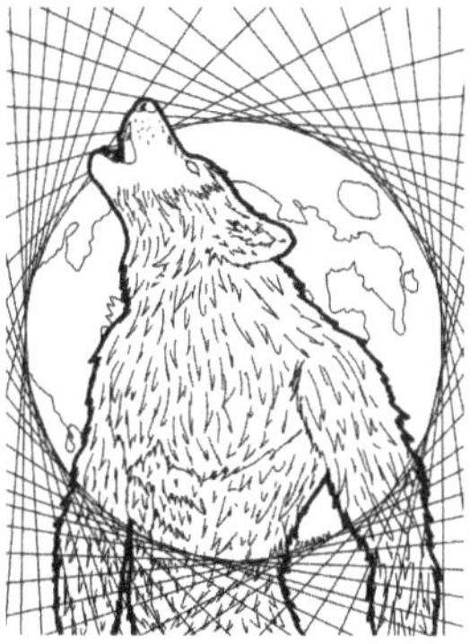
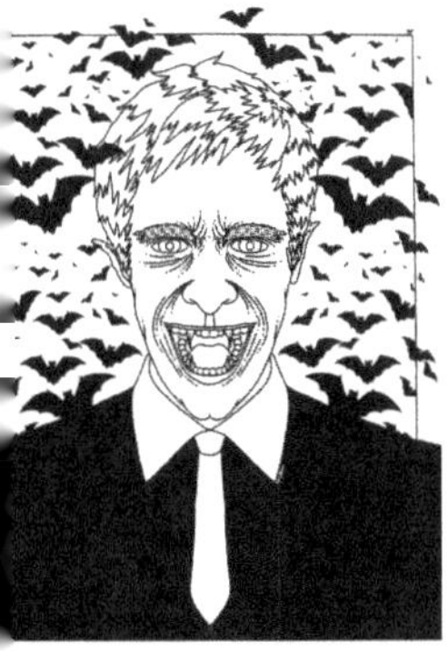
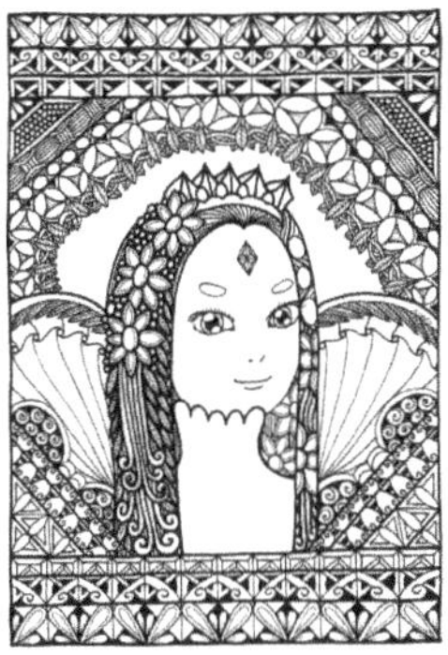
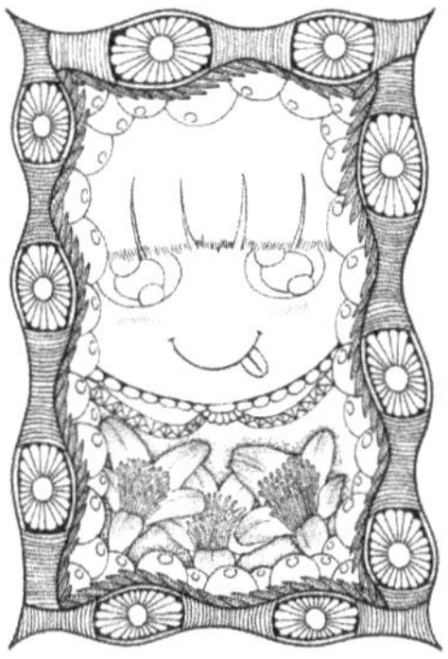
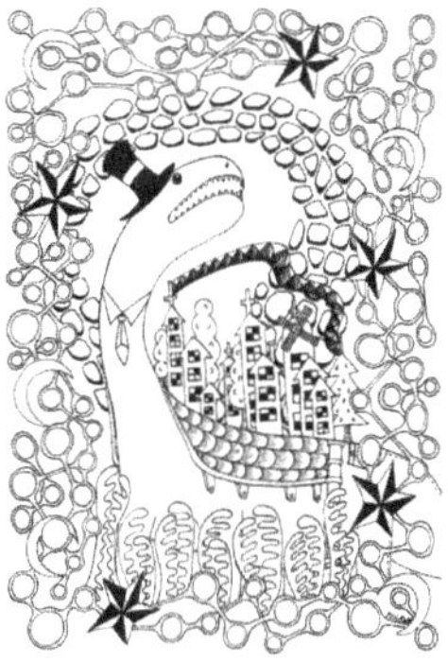
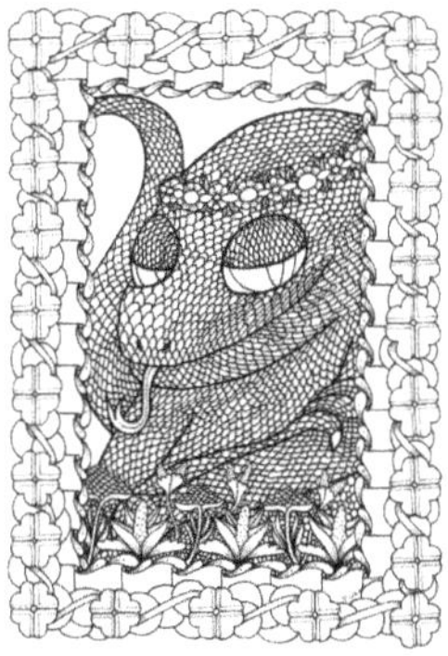
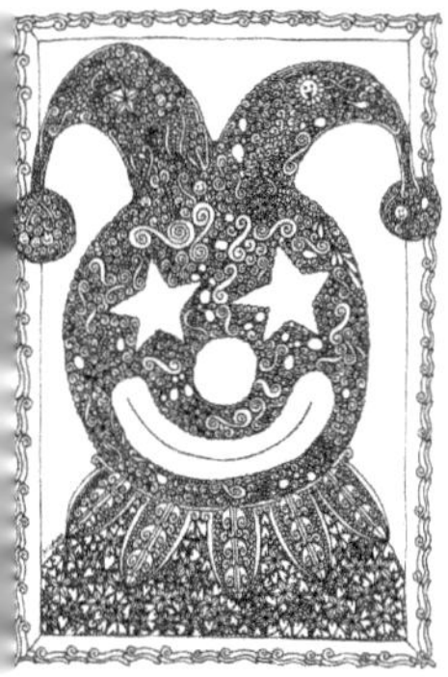
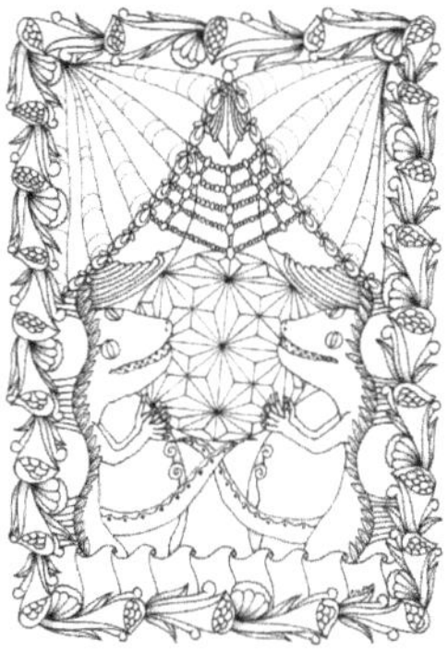
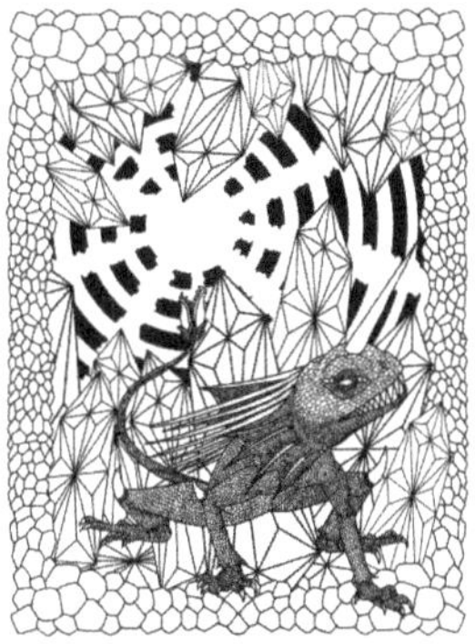
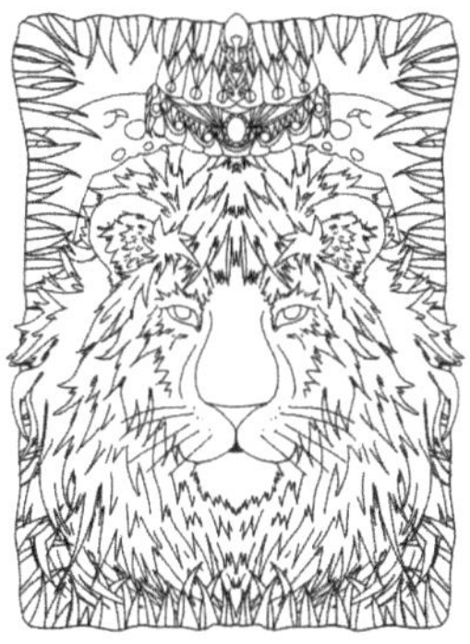
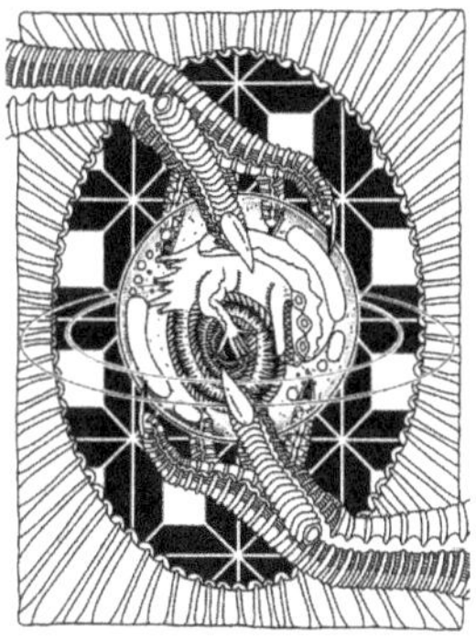
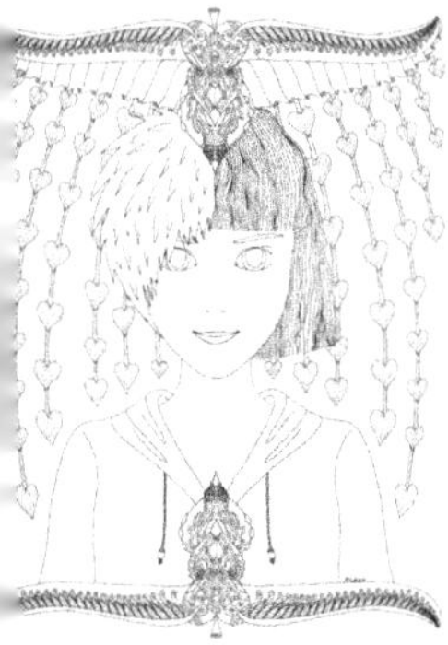
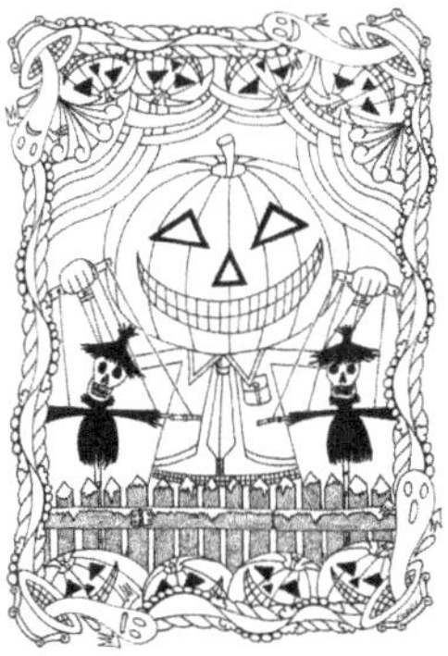
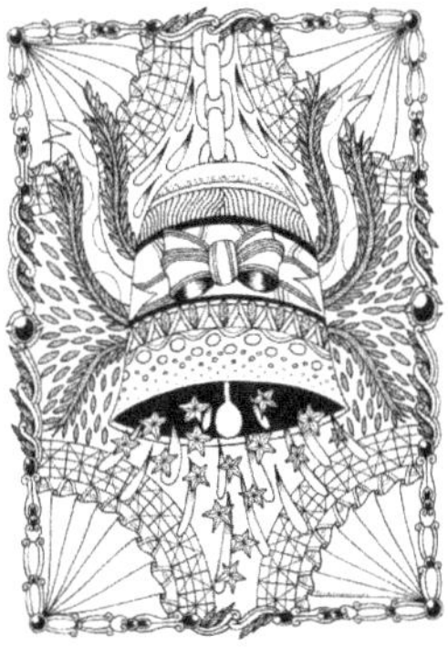
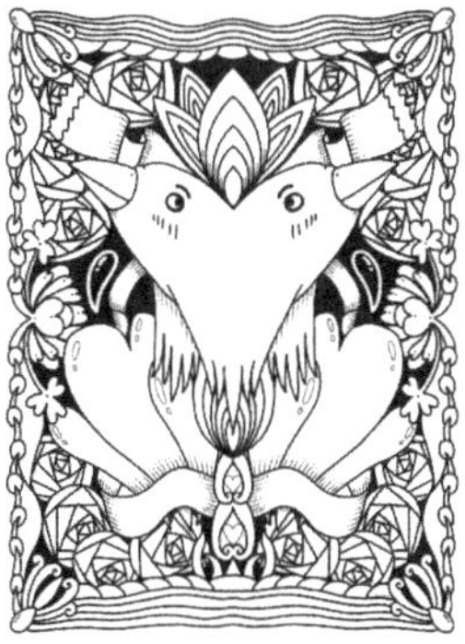
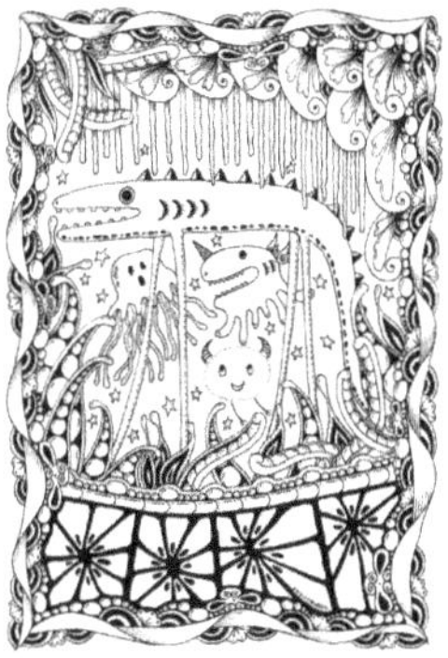
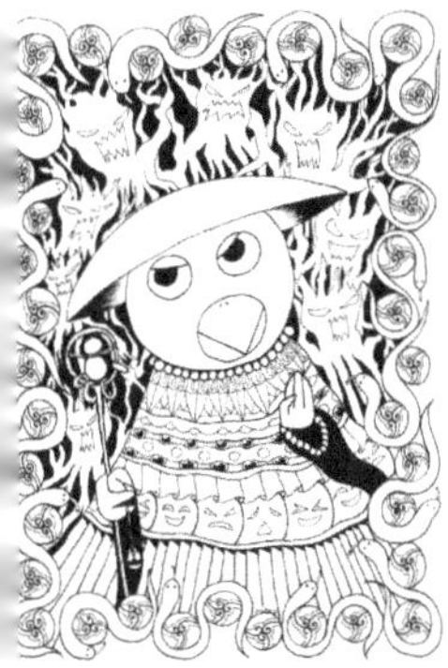
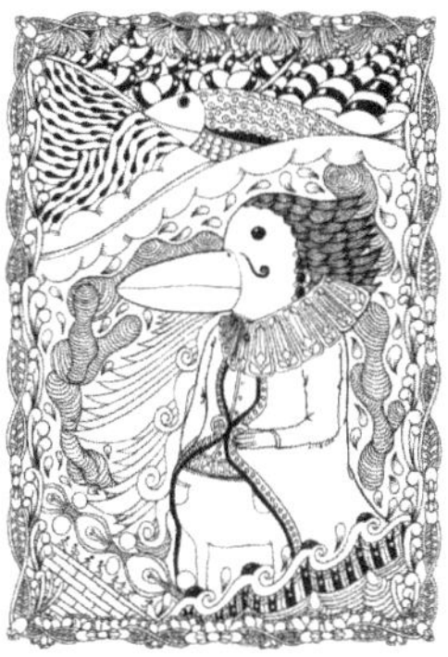
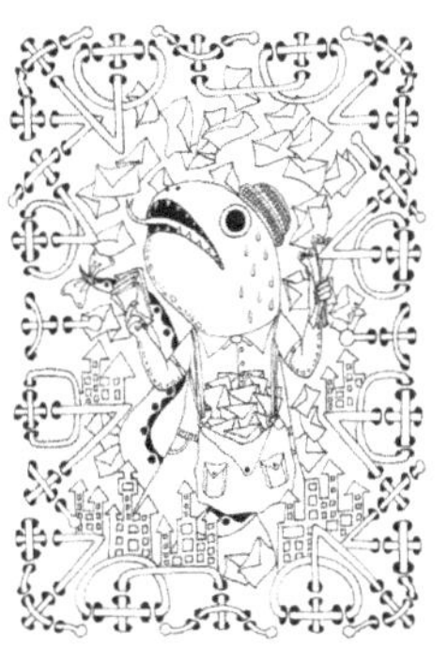
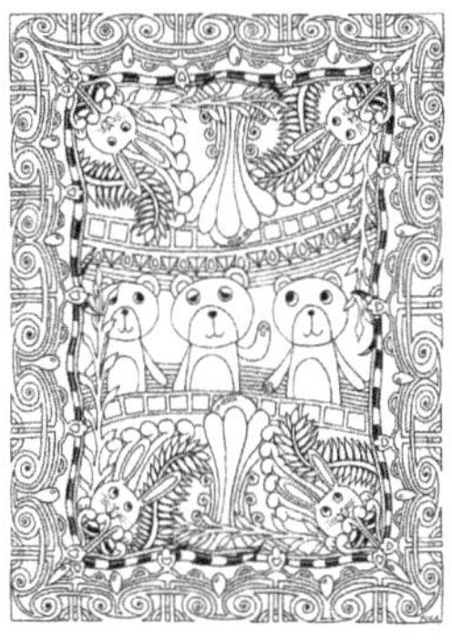
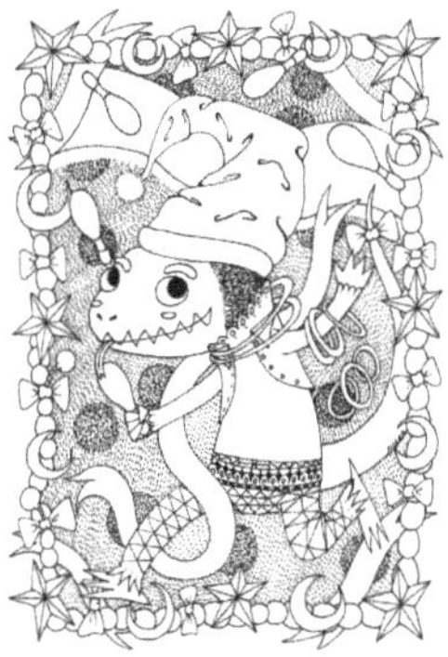

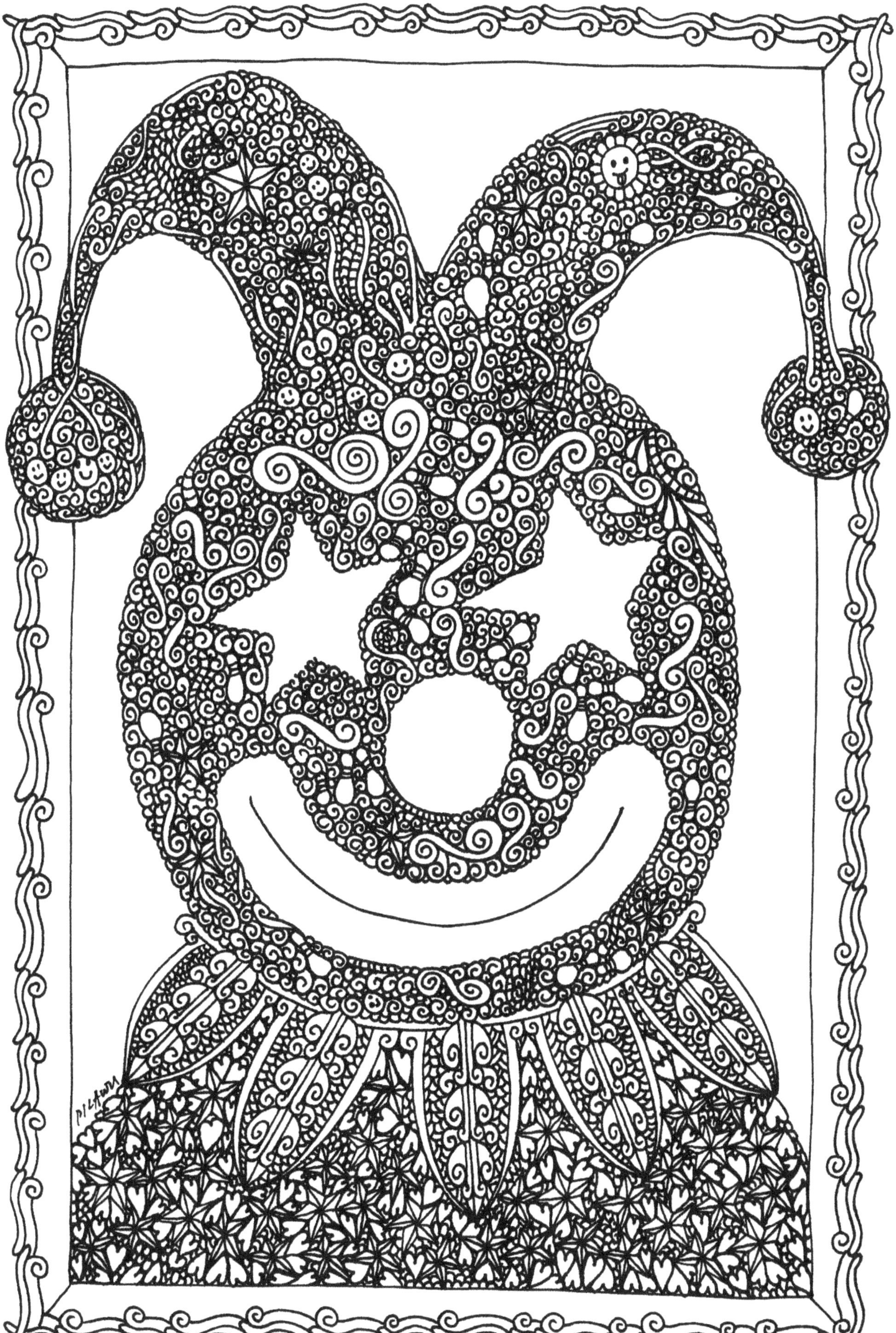

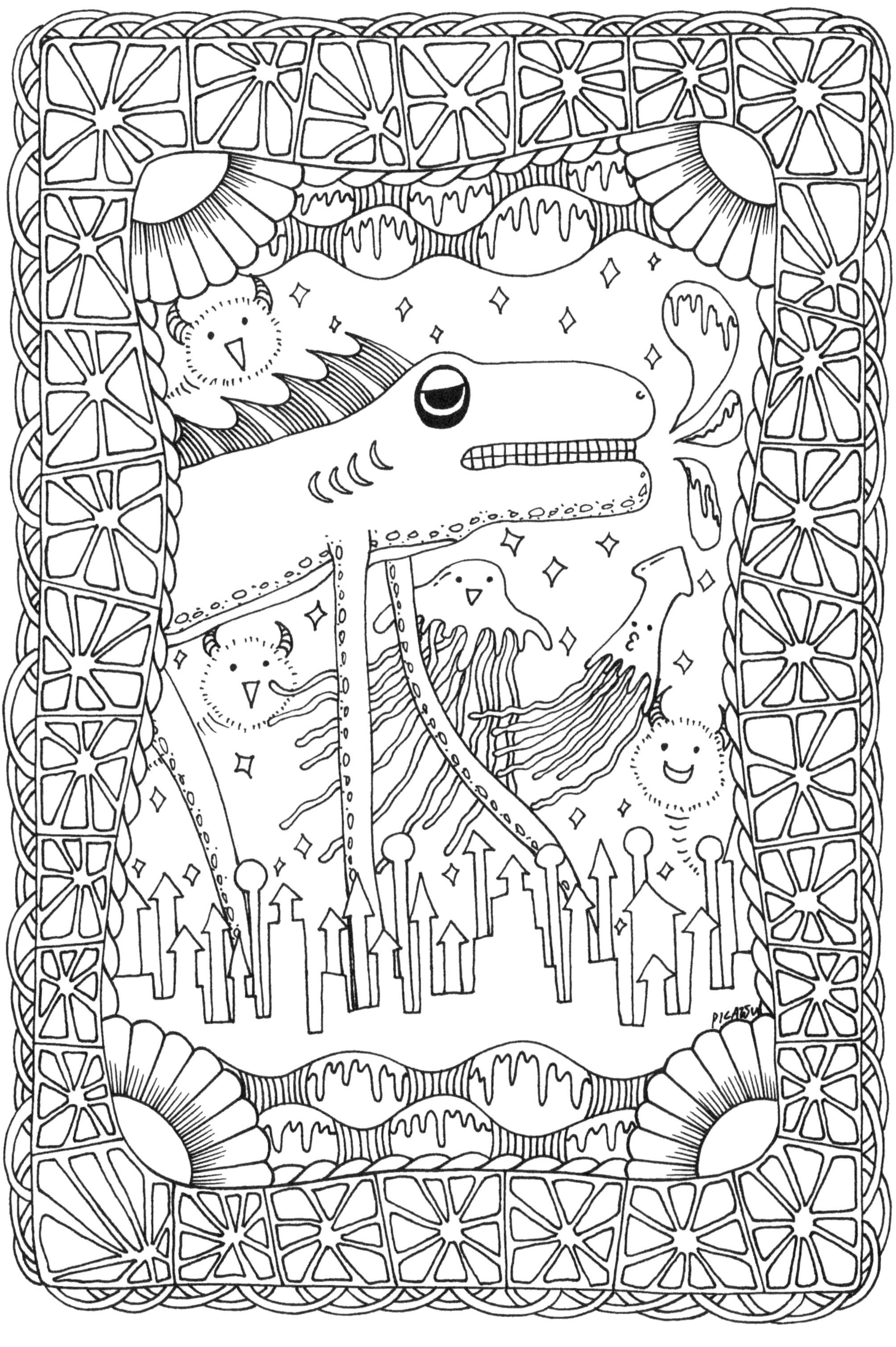

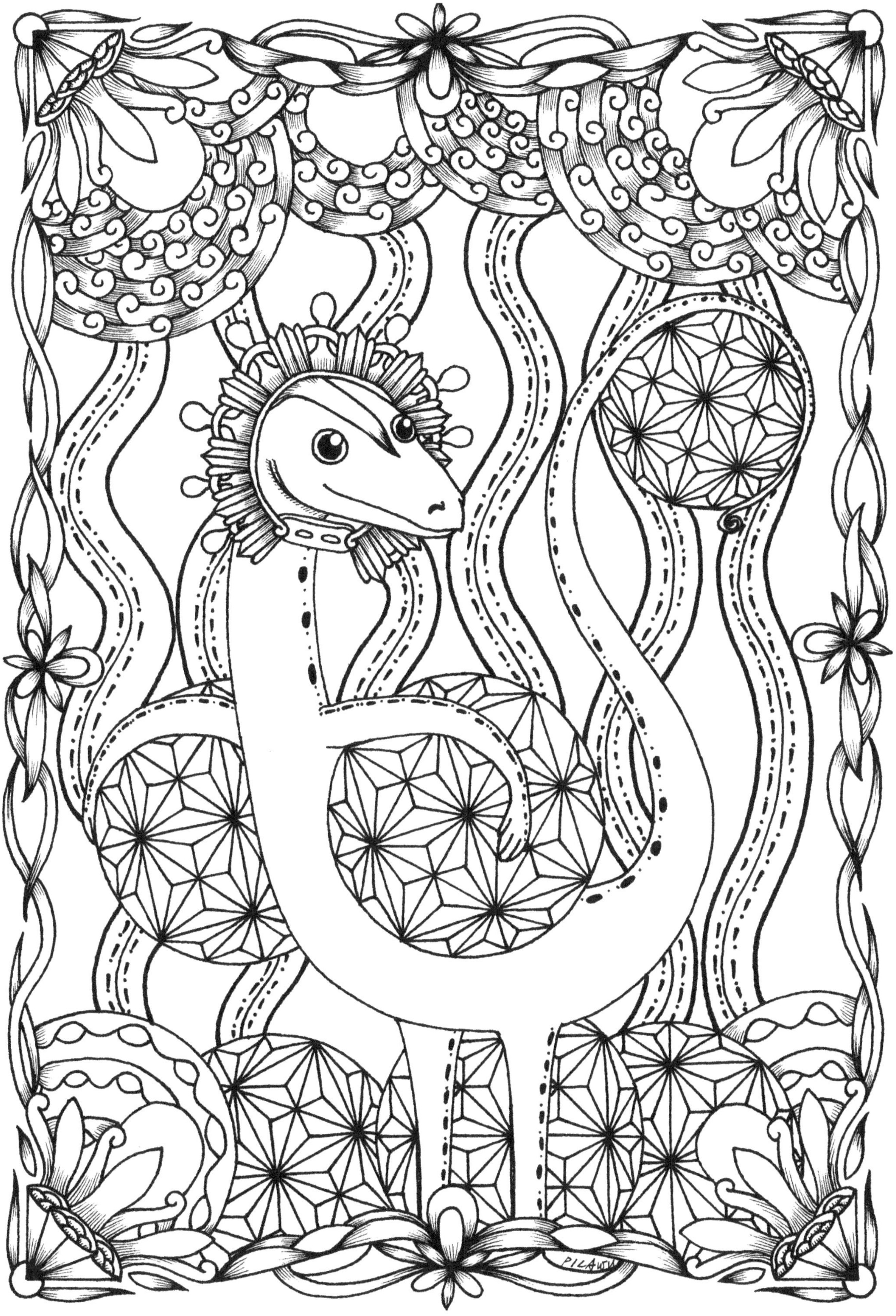

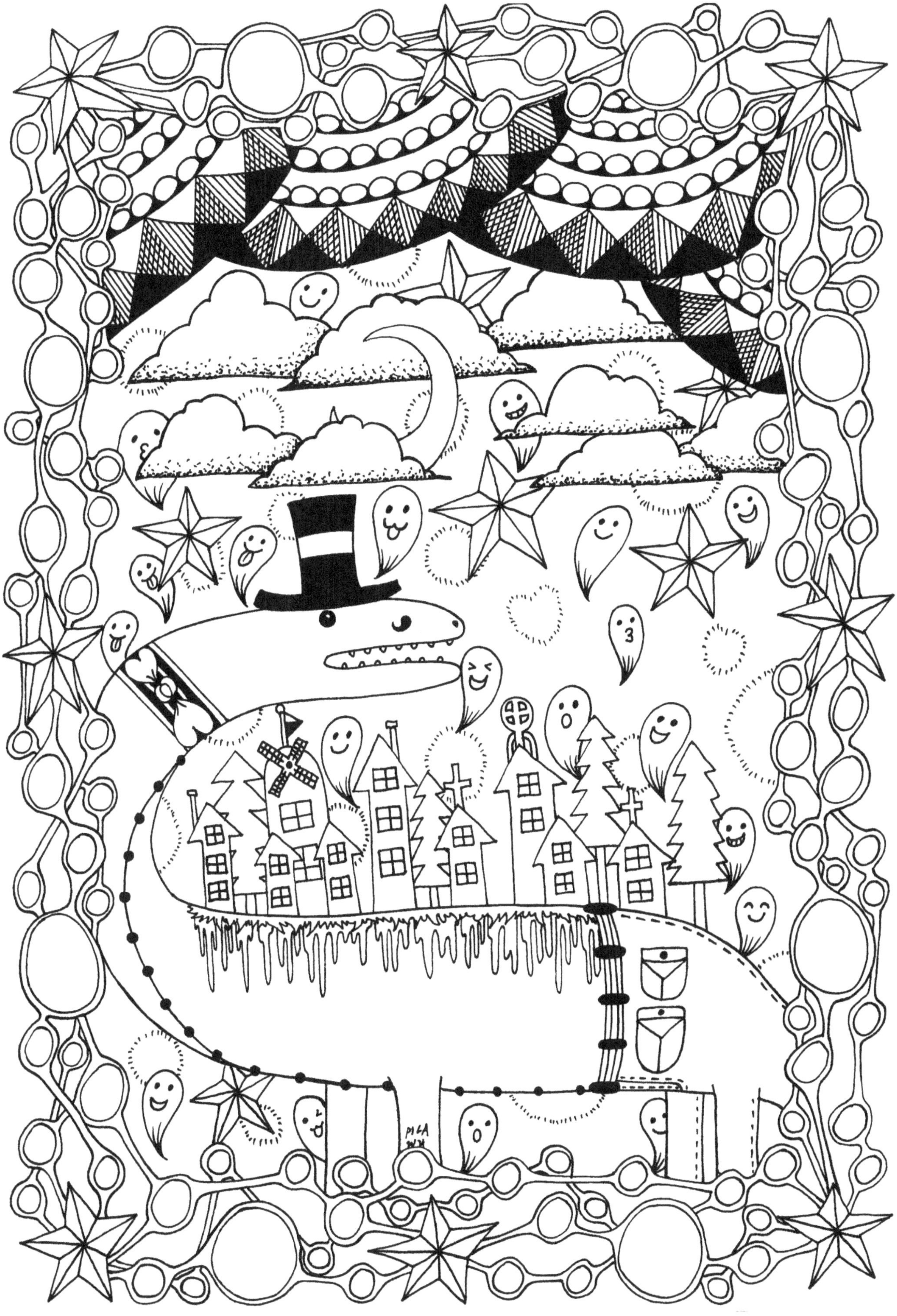

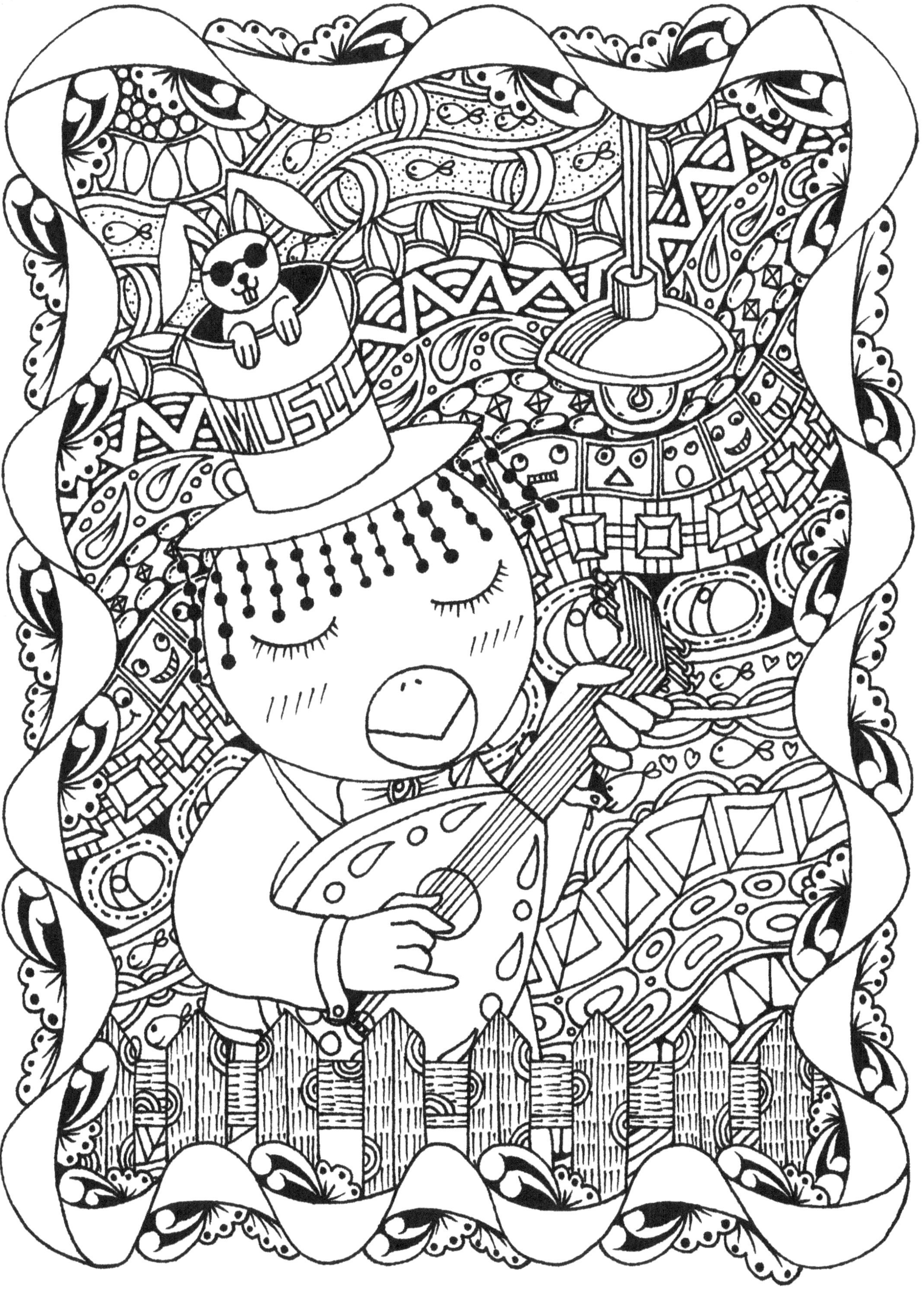
MUSIC

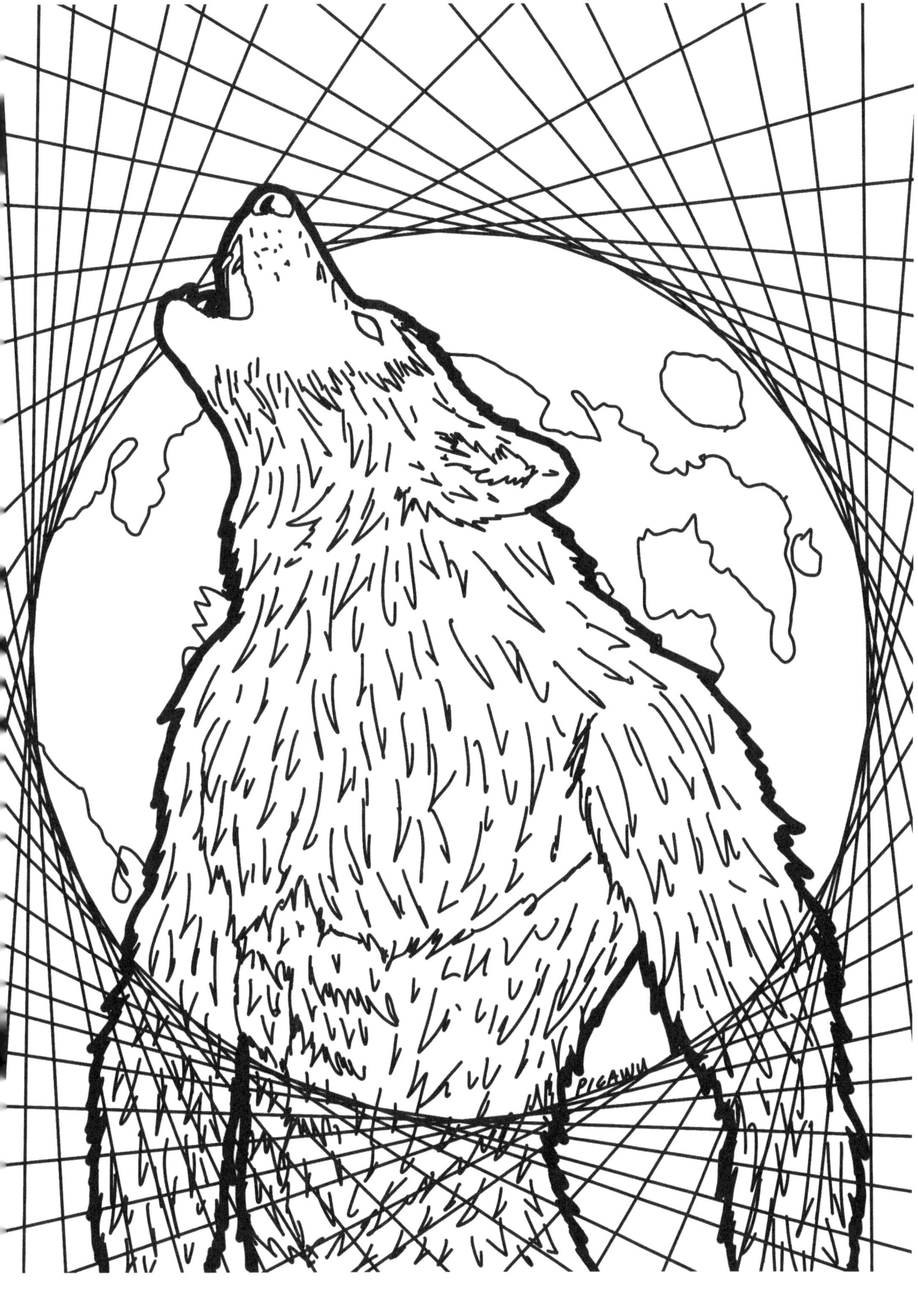
PICAWU

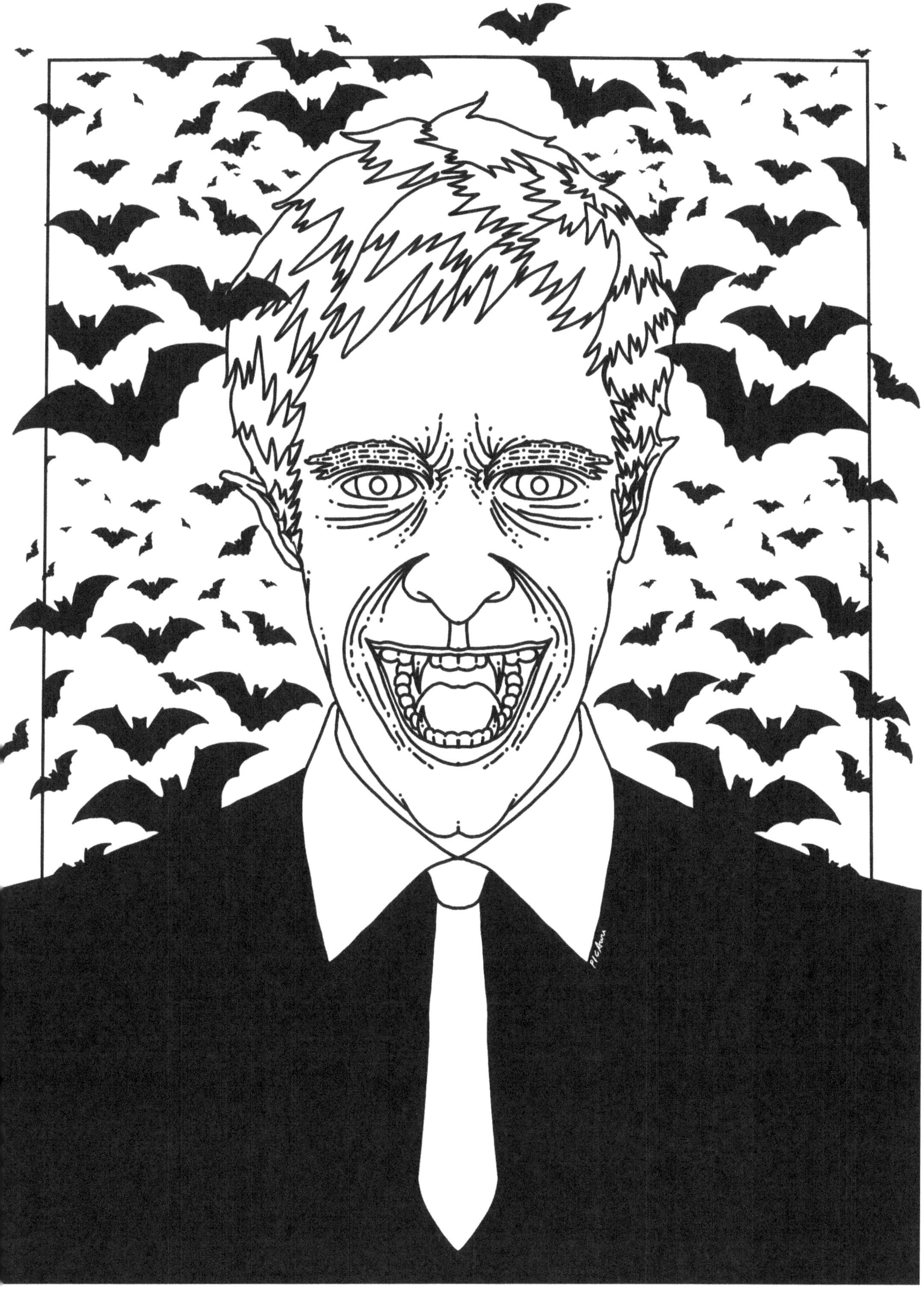

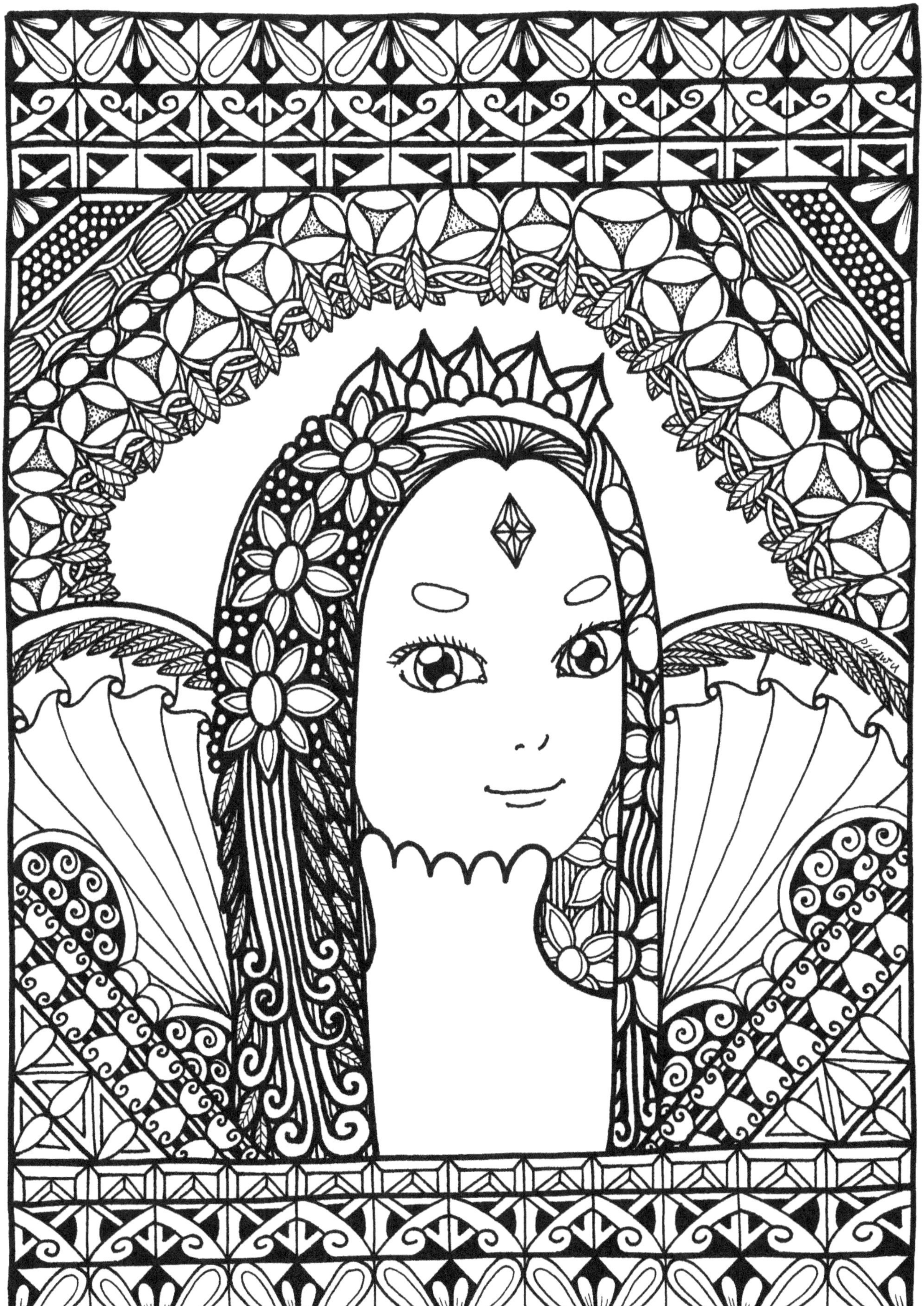

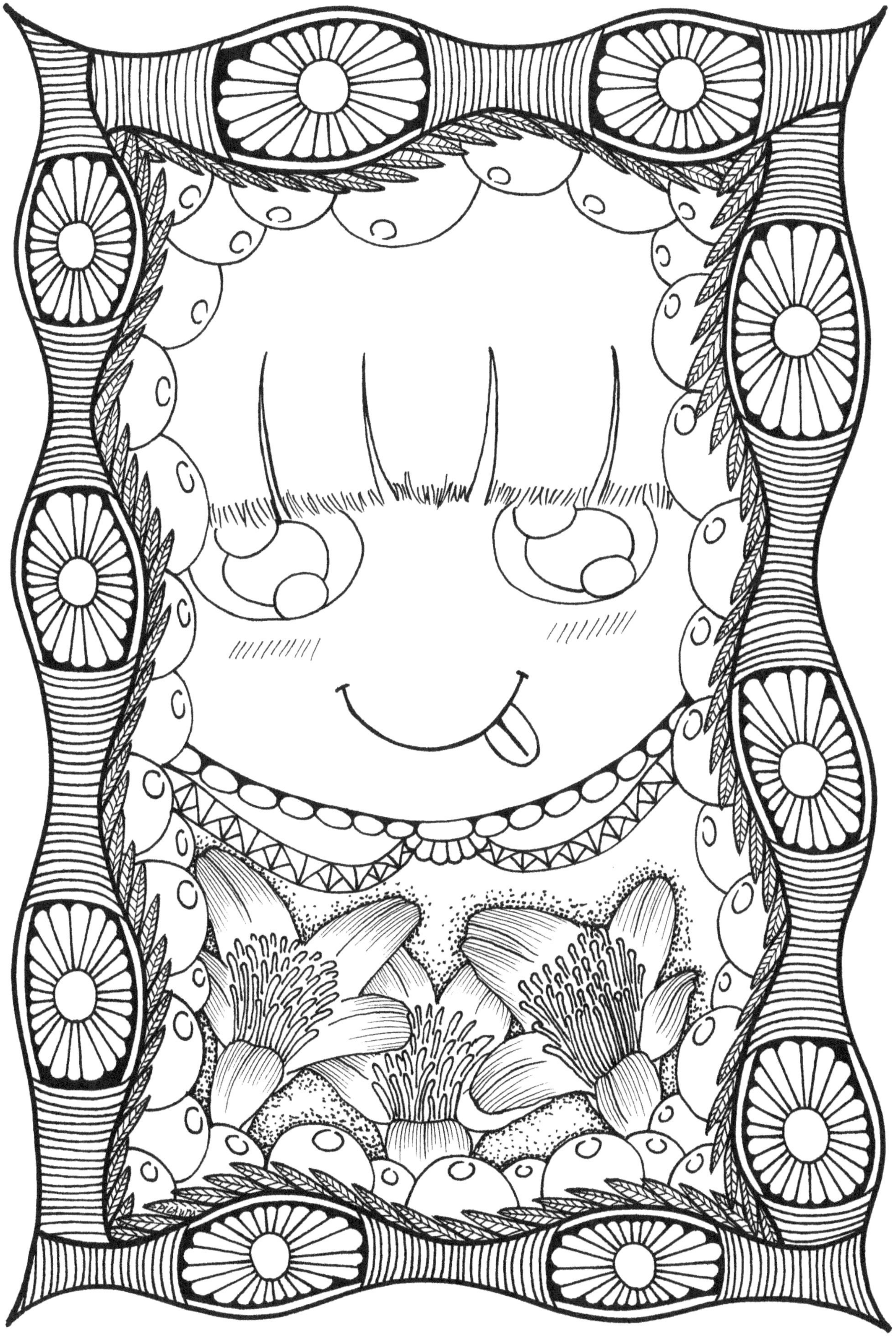

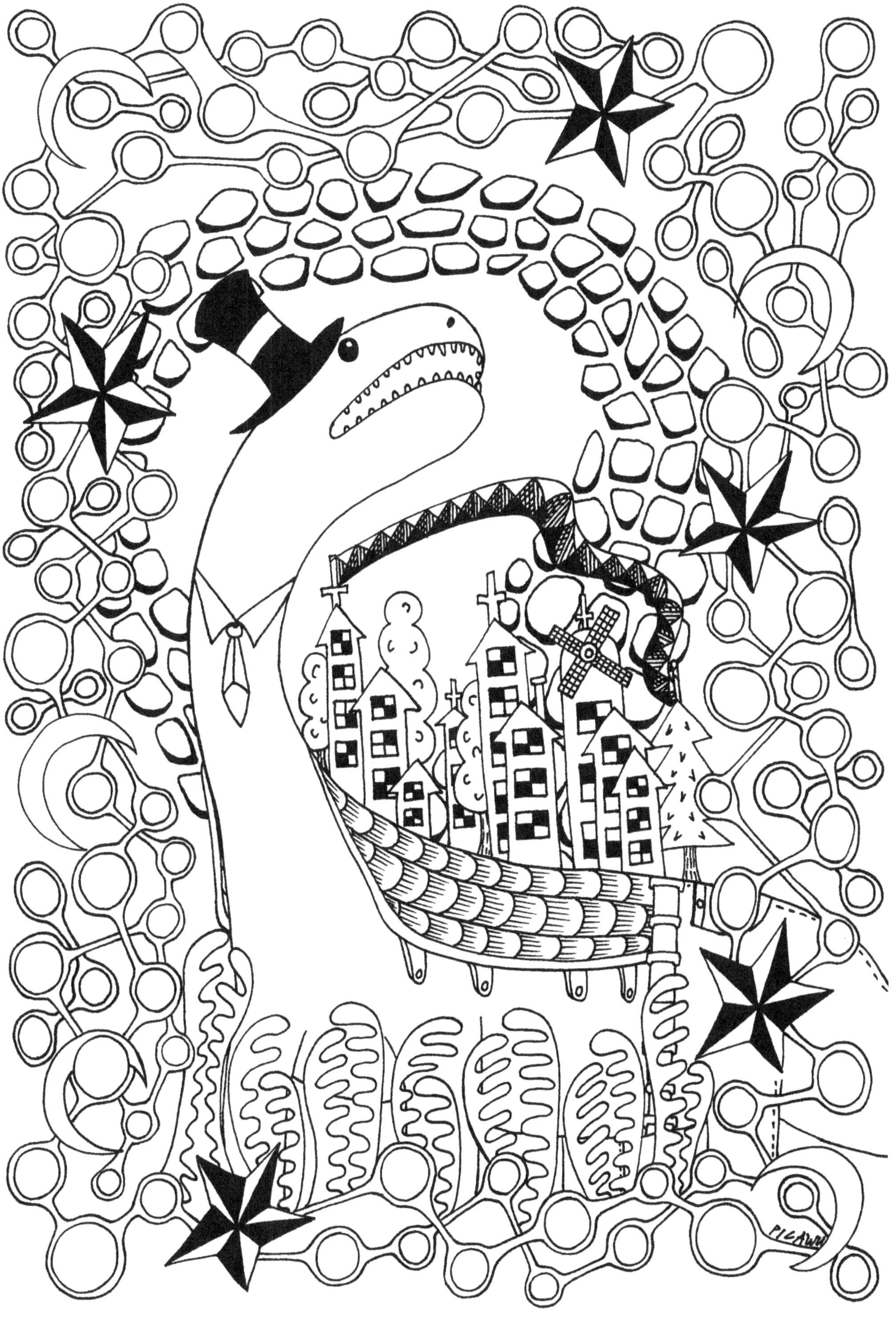

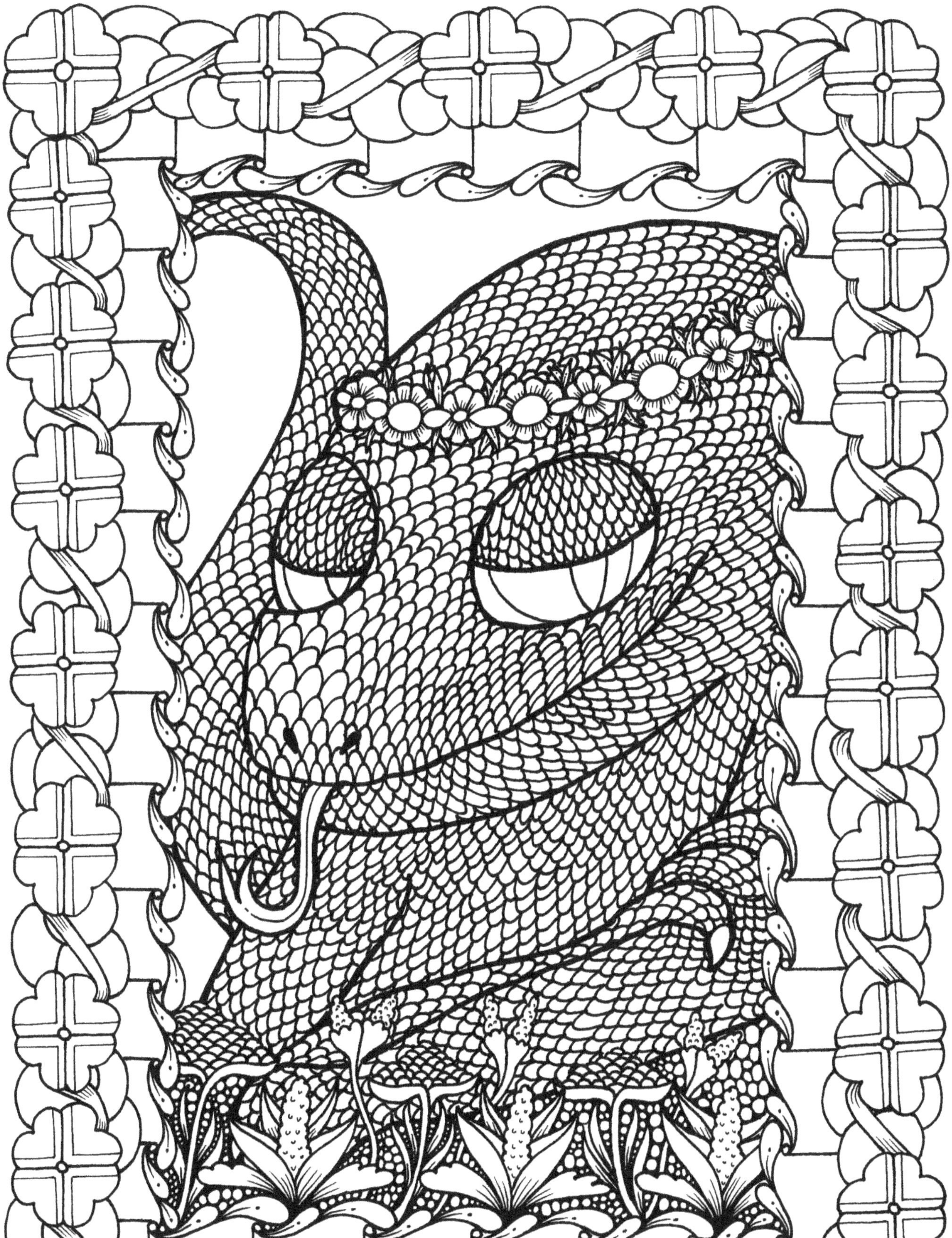

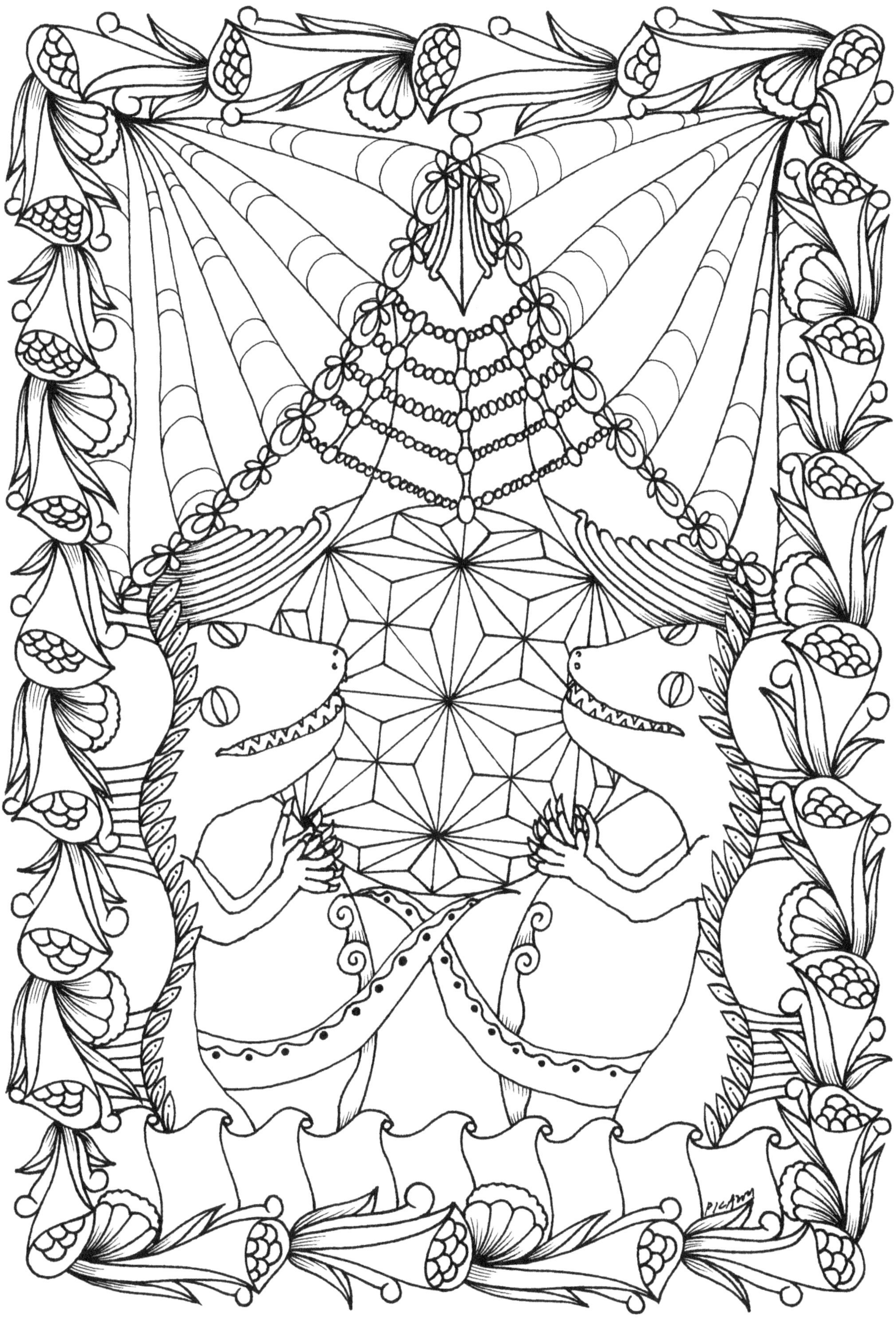

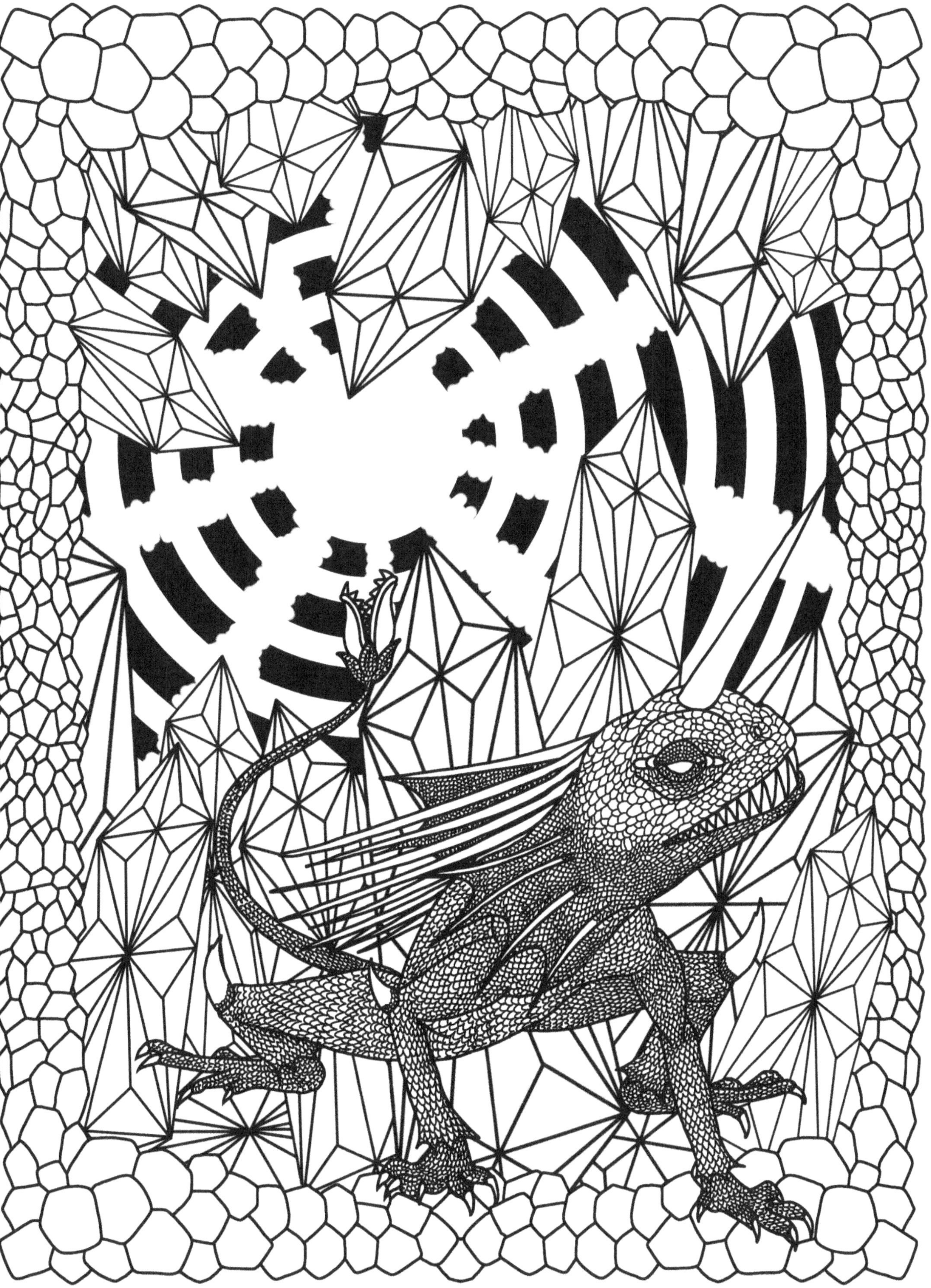

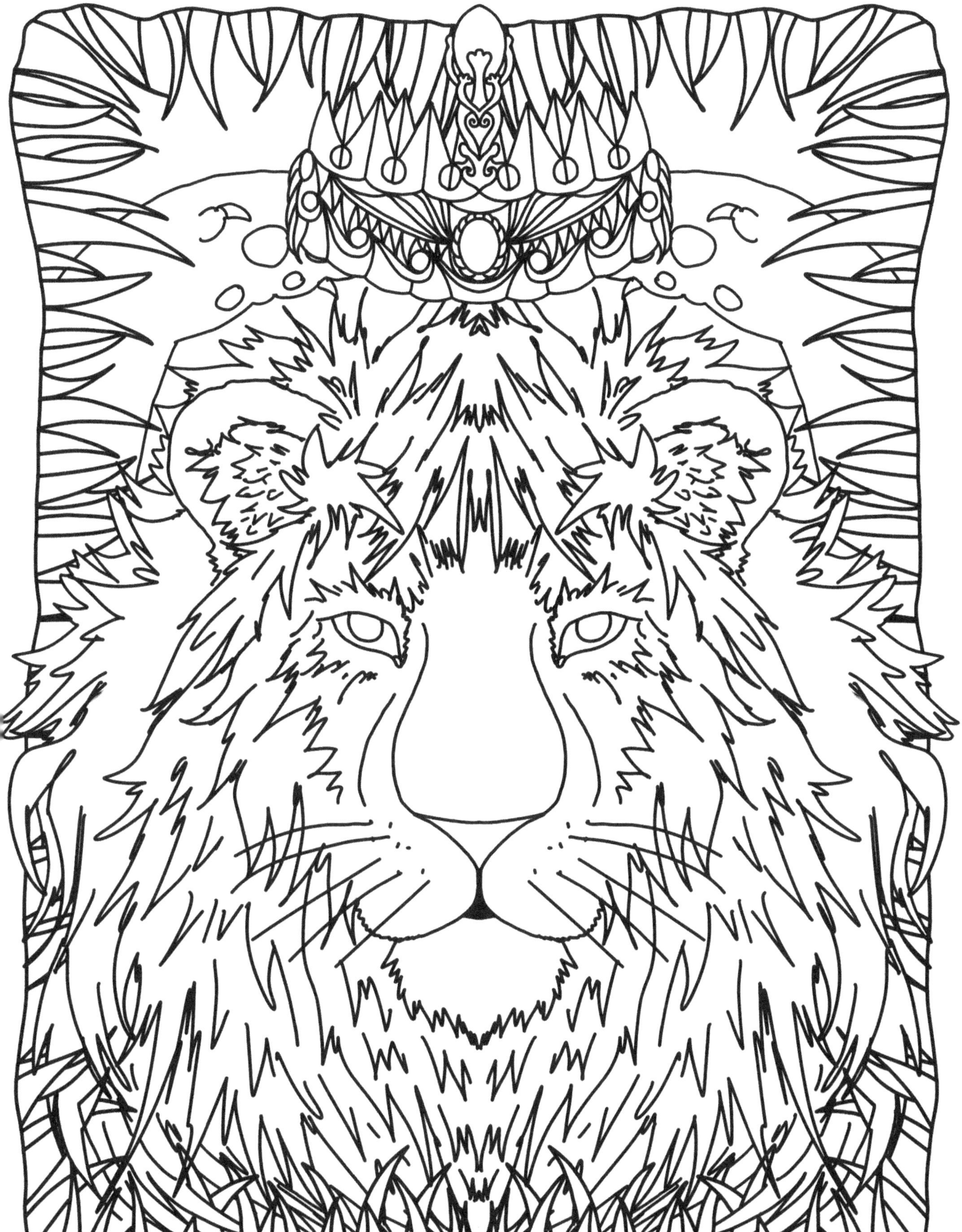

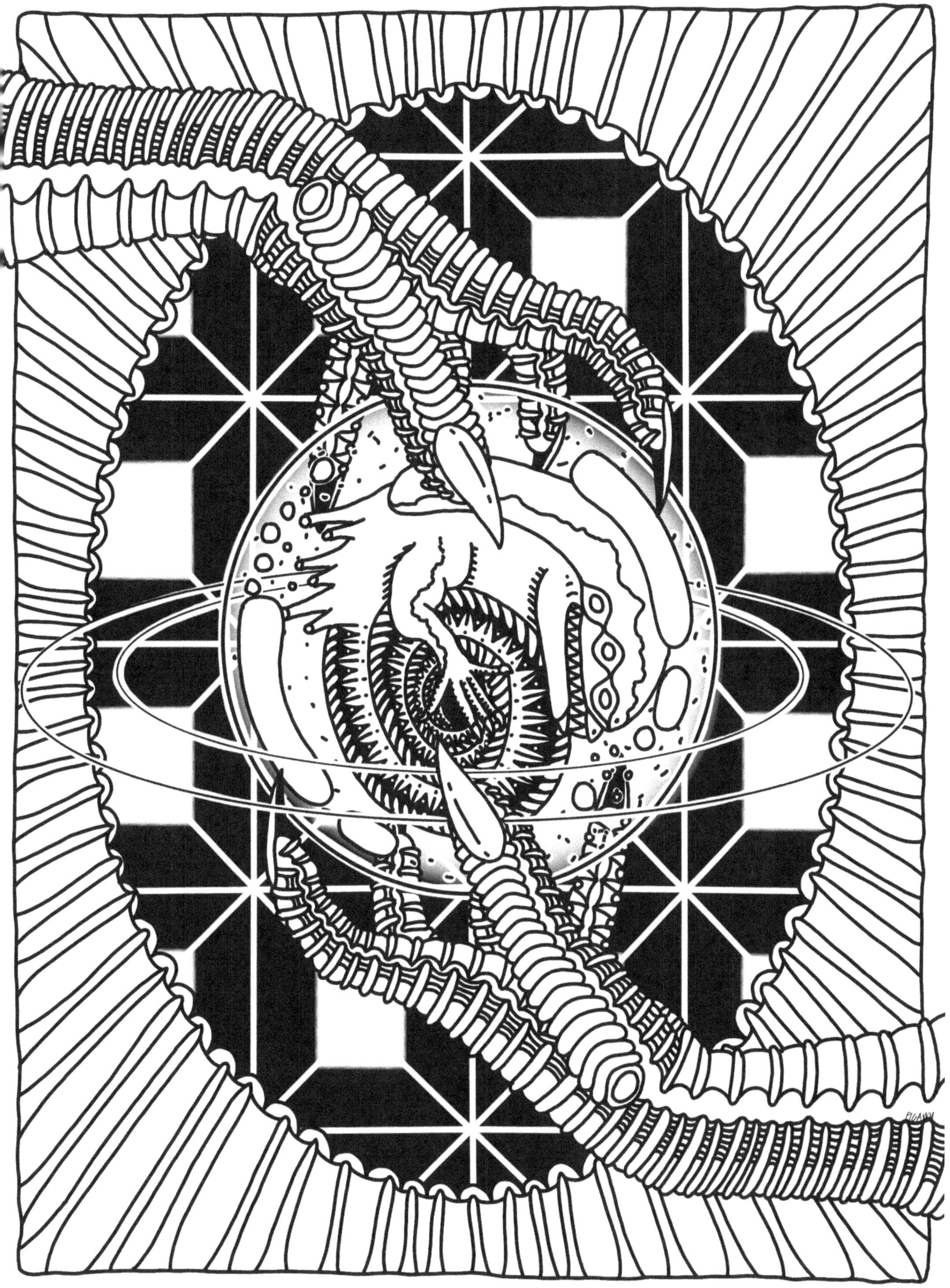

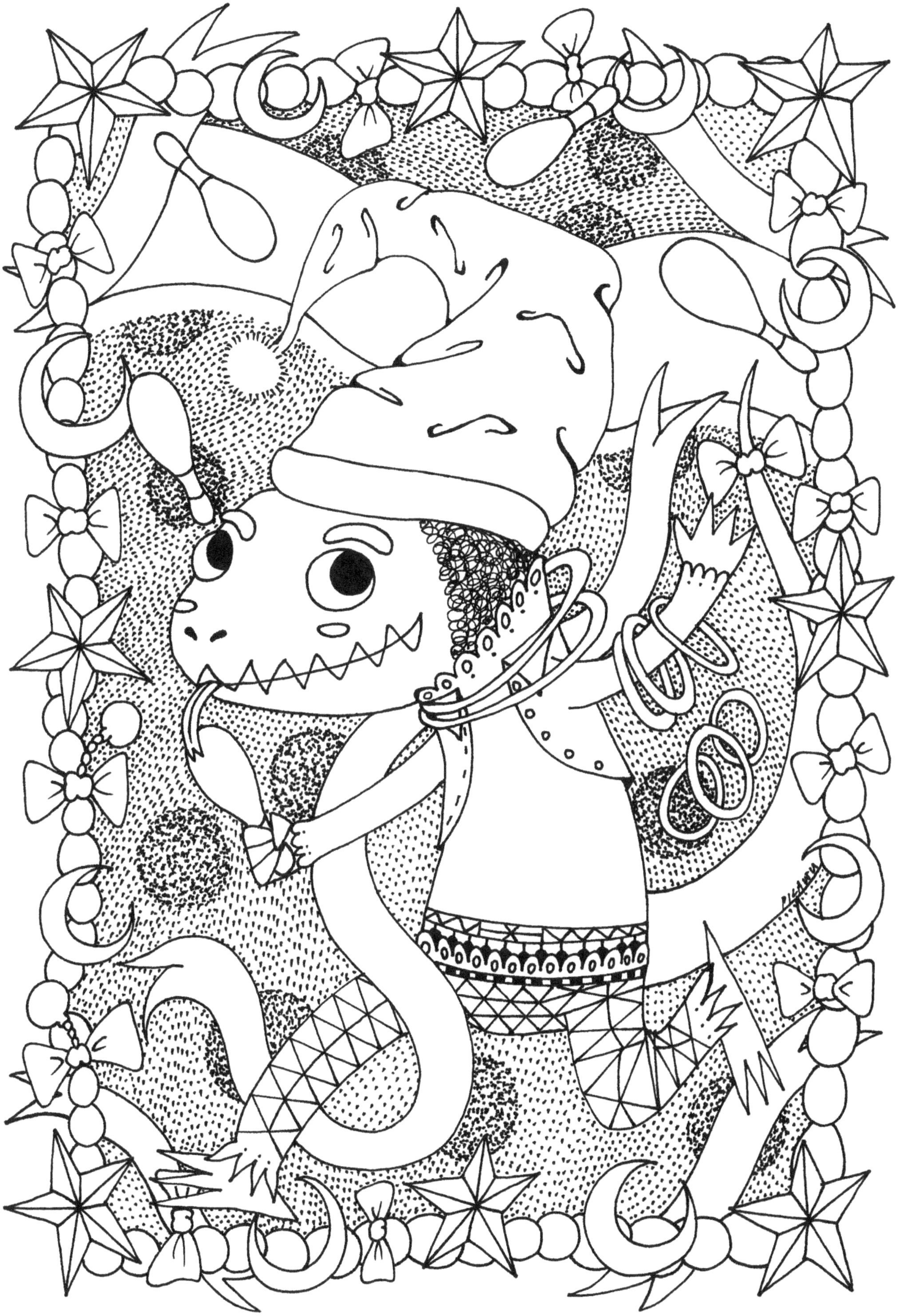

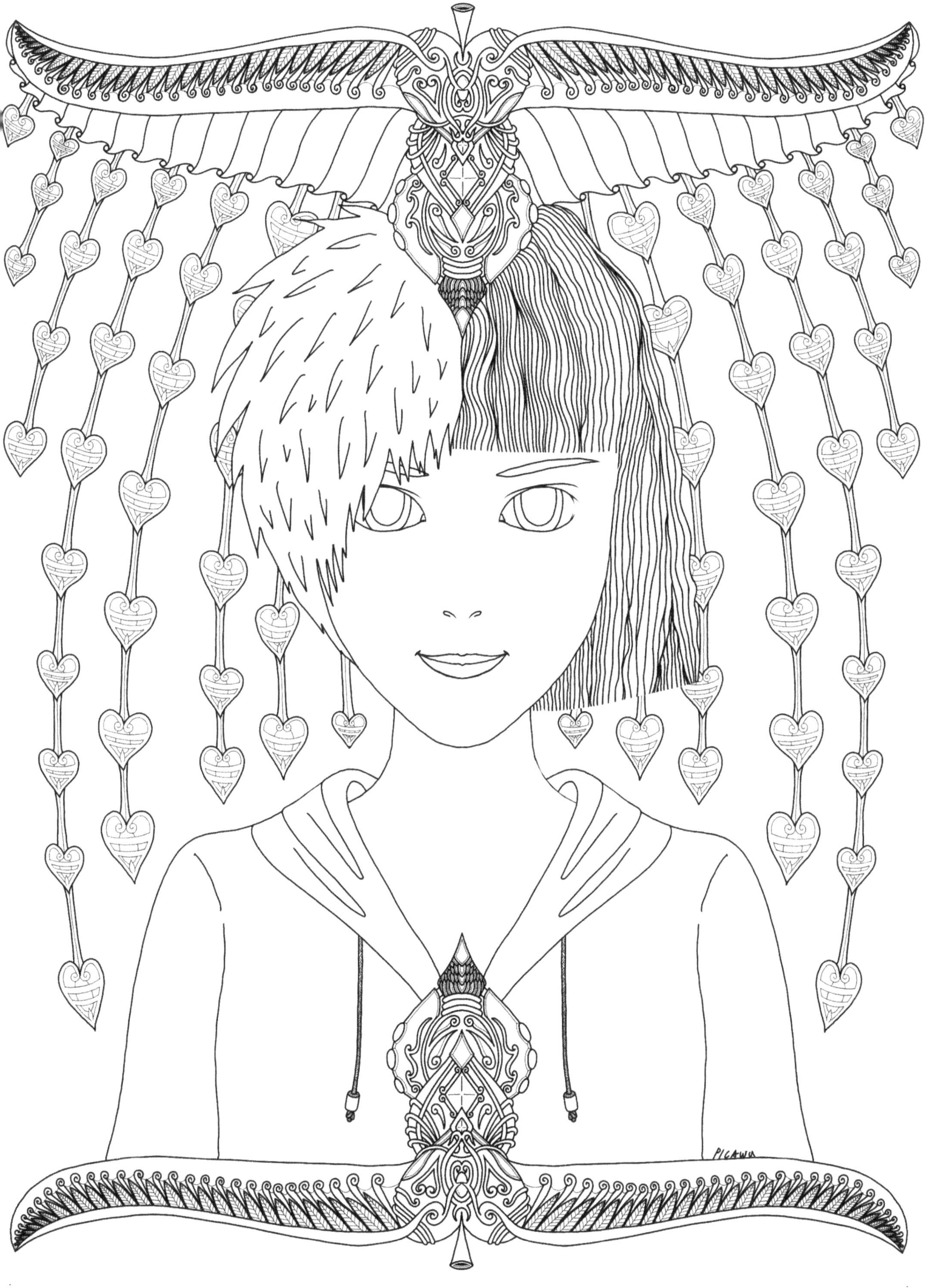
PICAWU

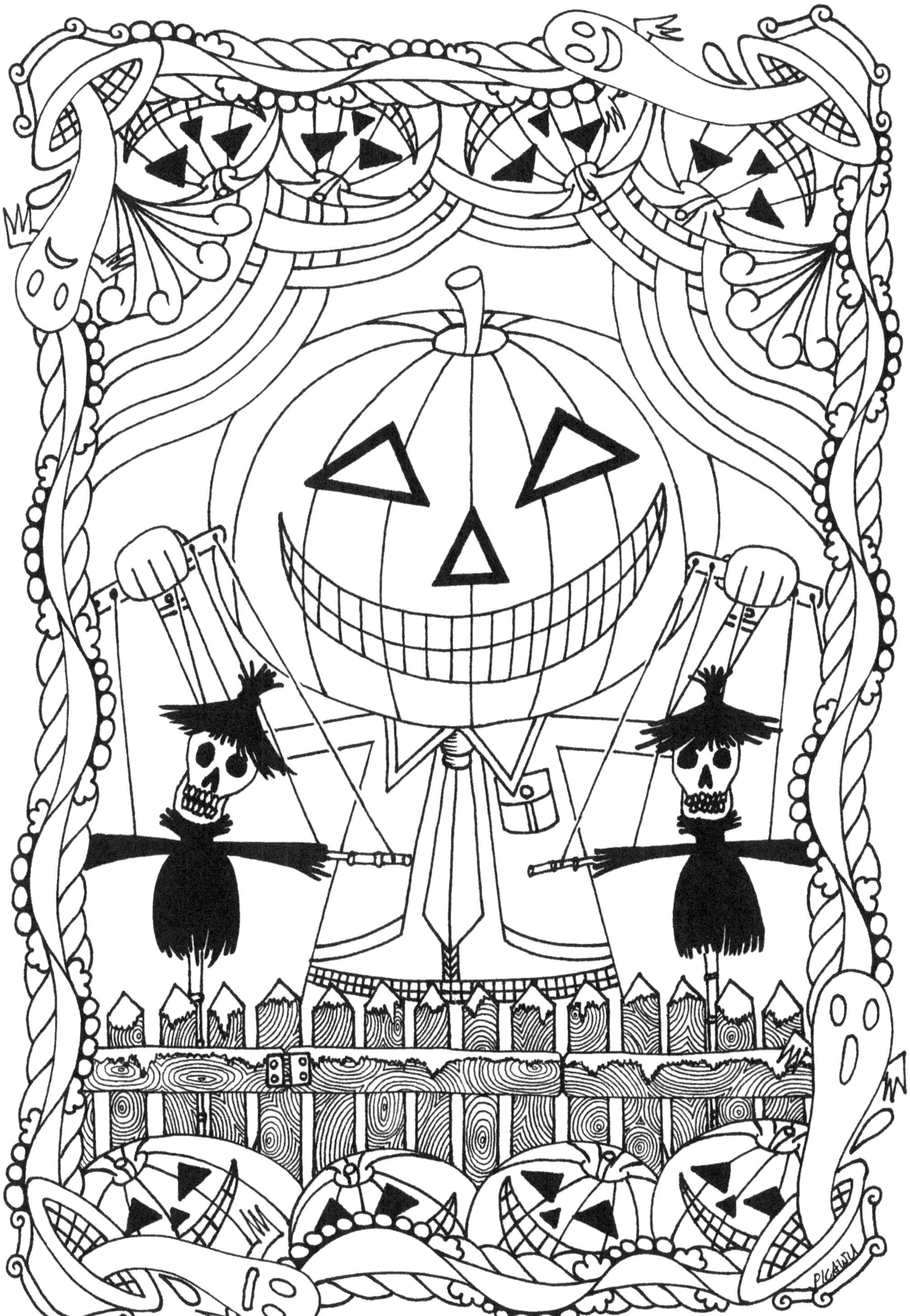

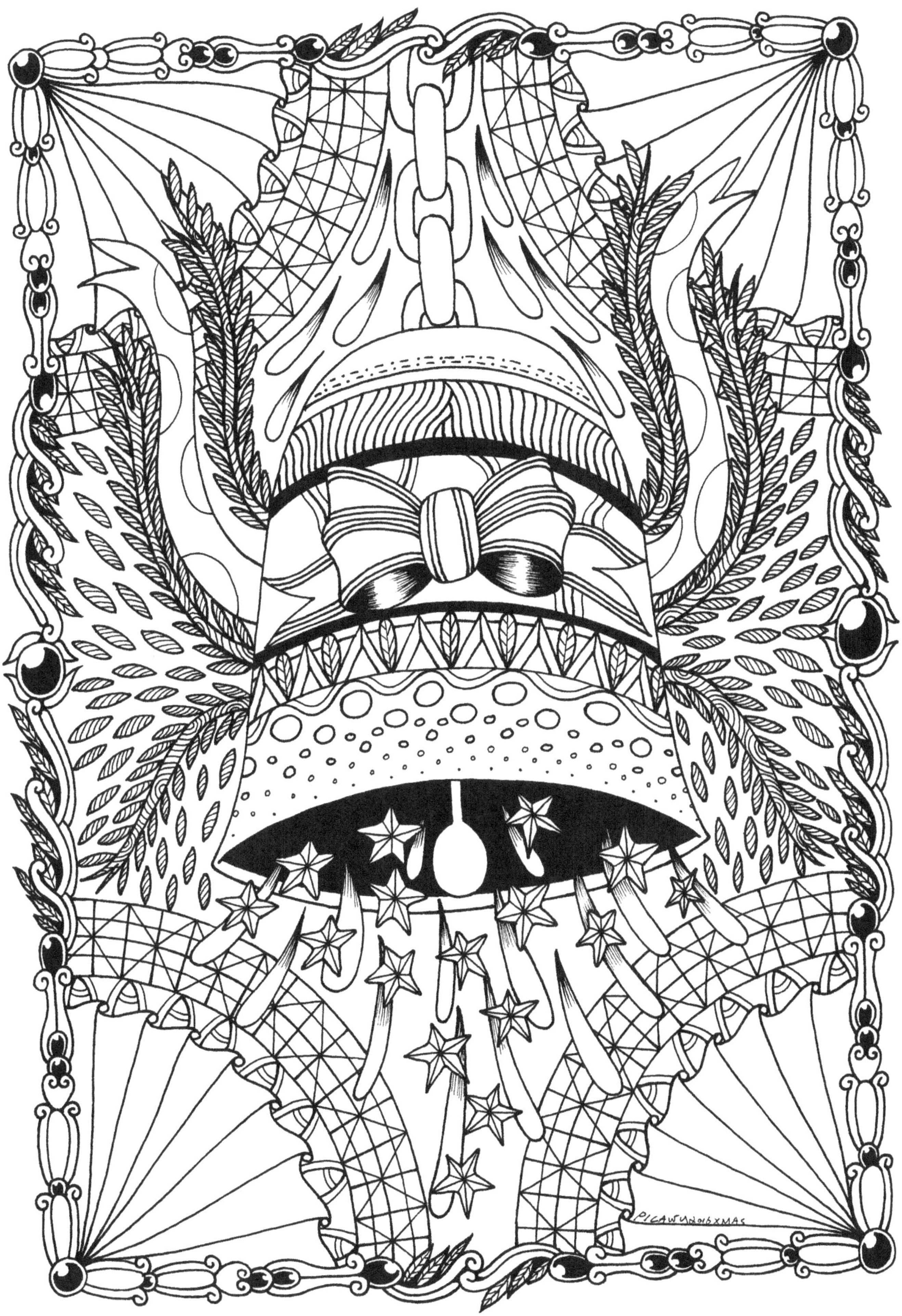
PICAWYN2016XMAS

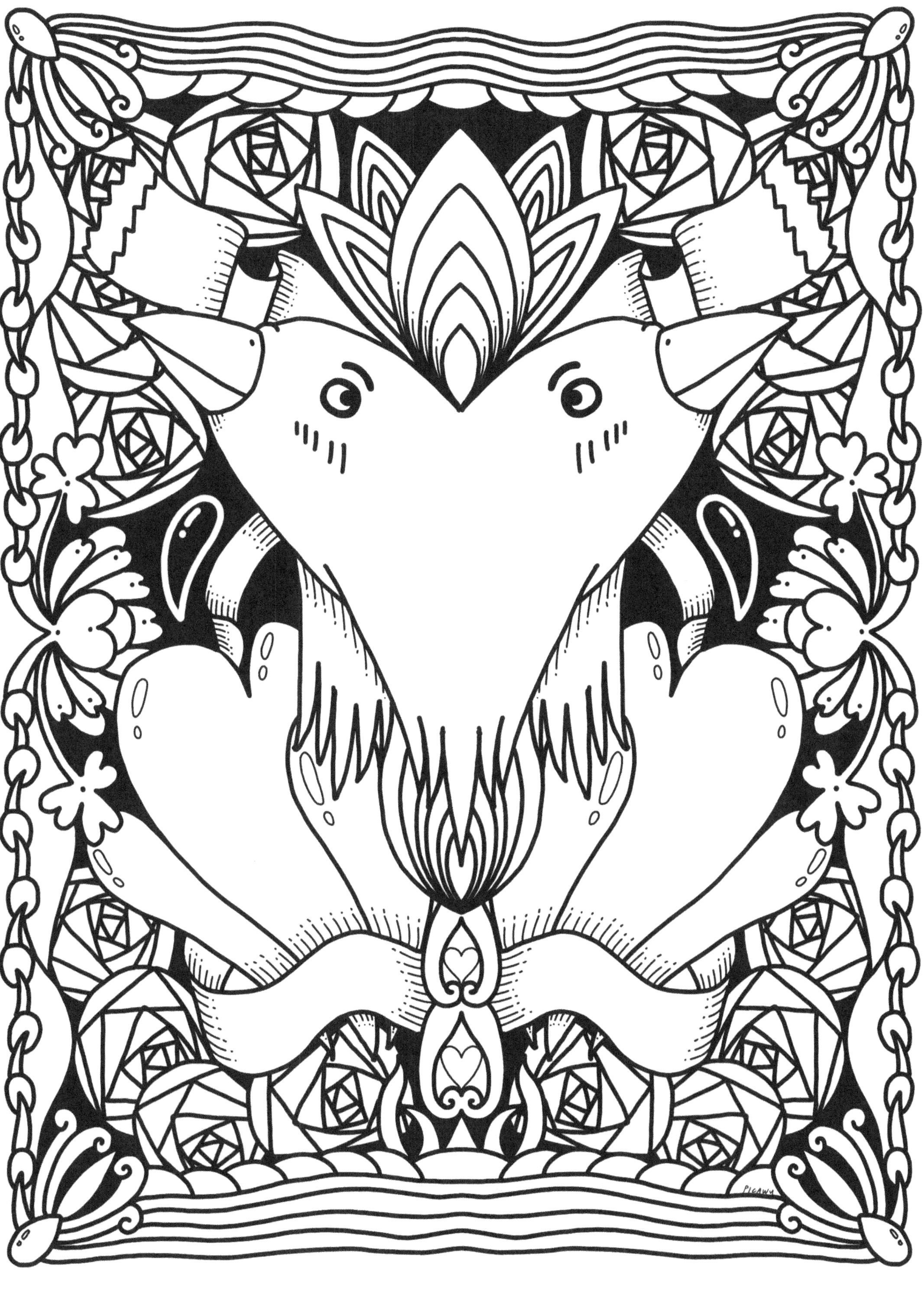
PIGAWY

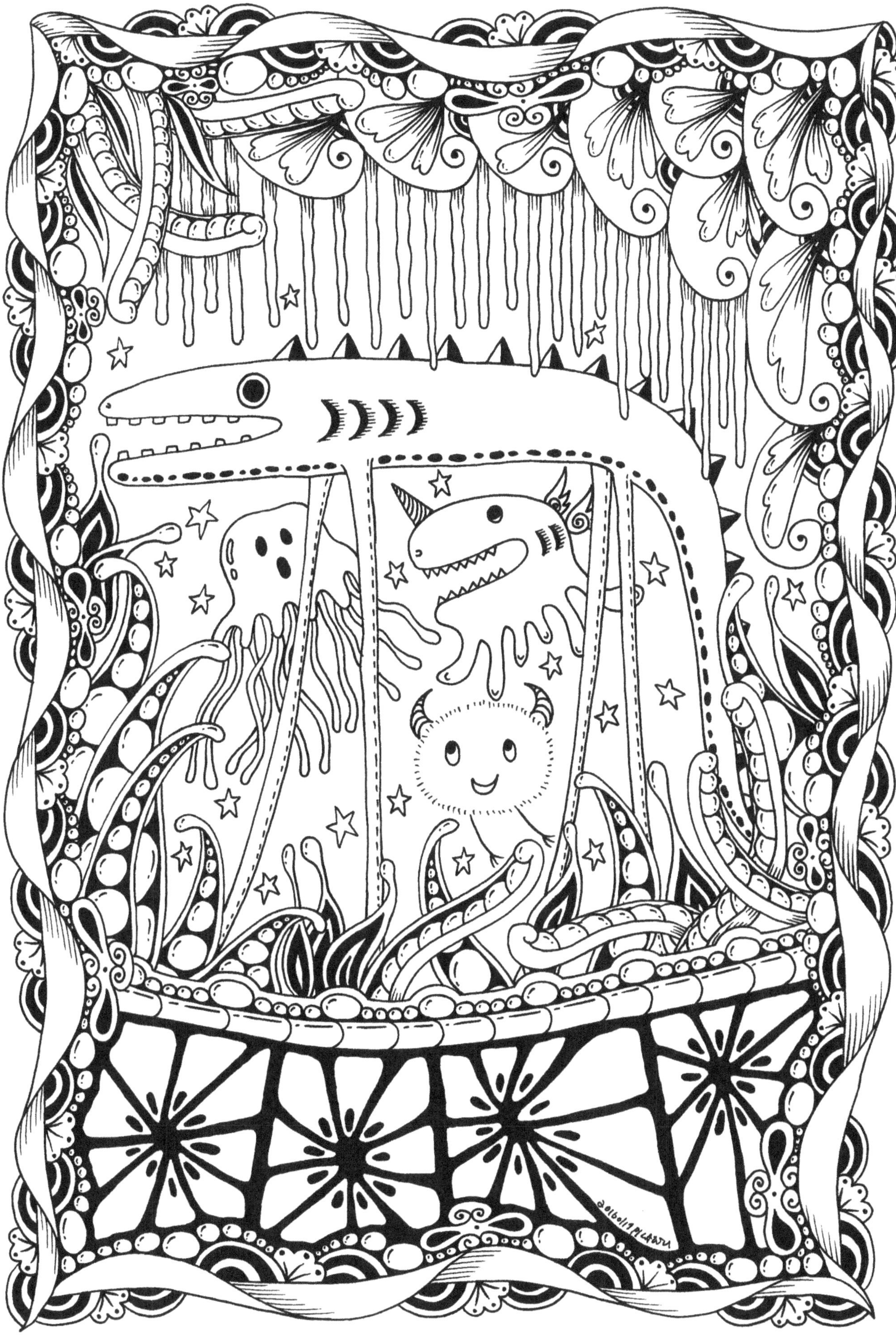

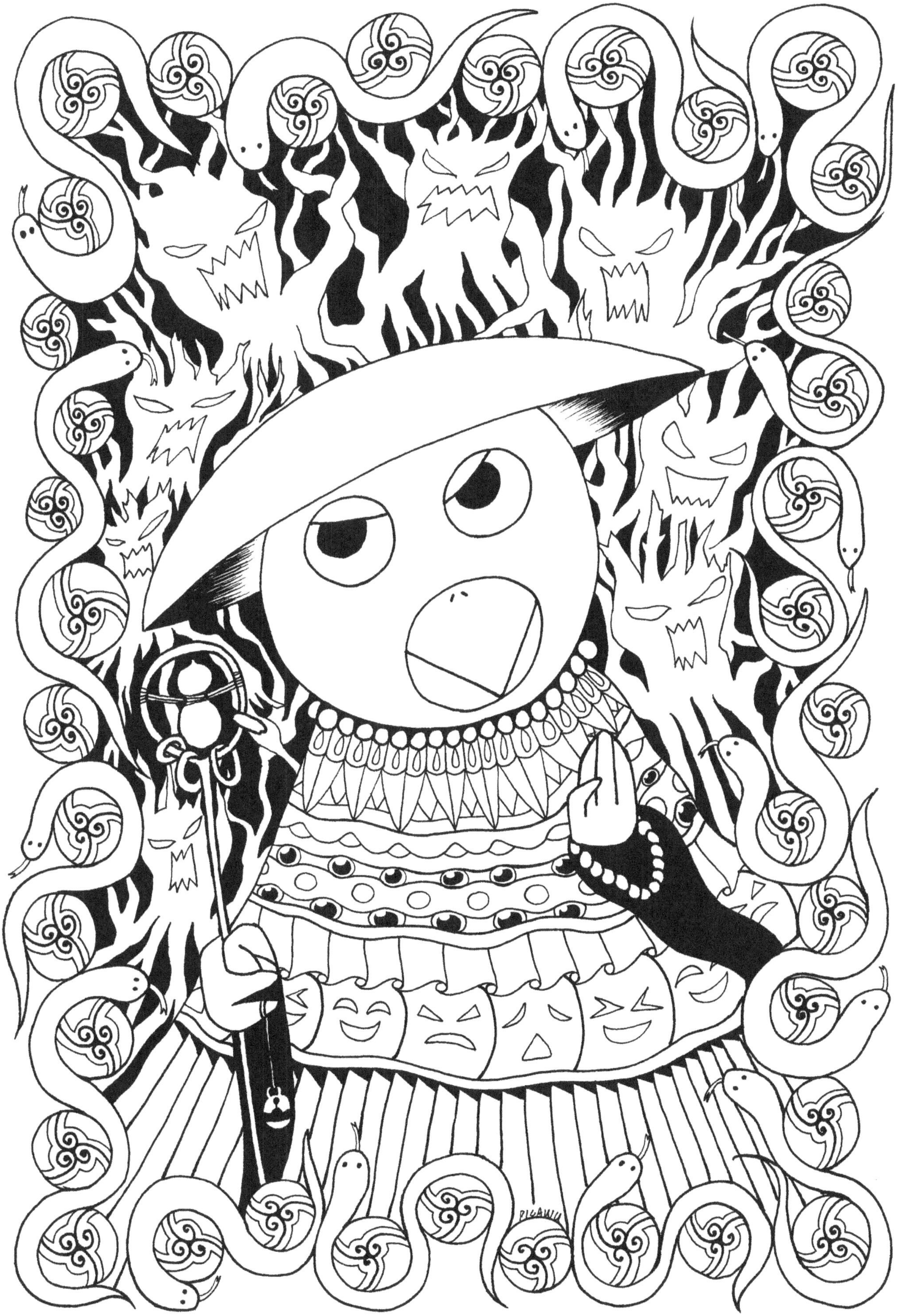

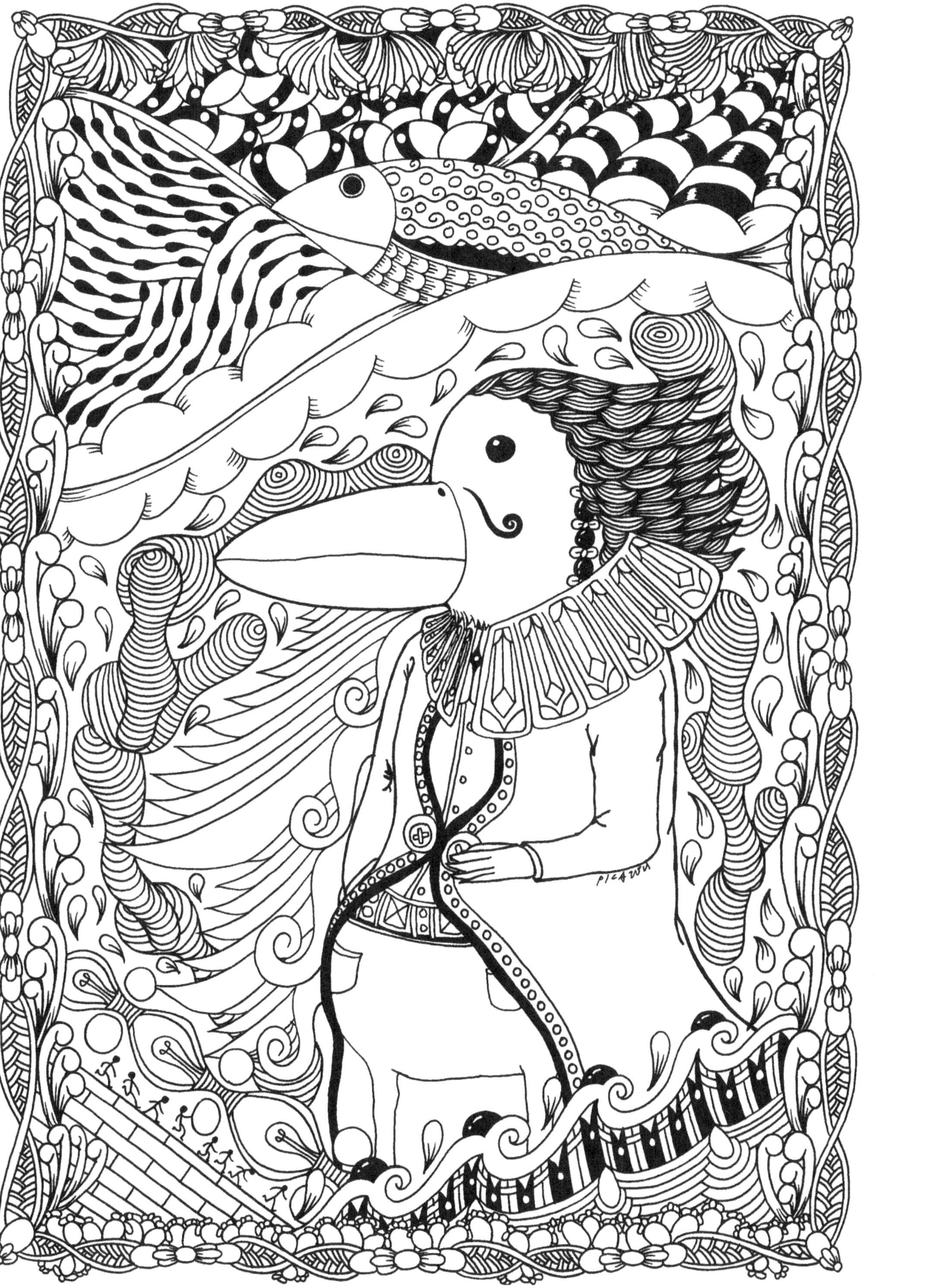
PICAWU

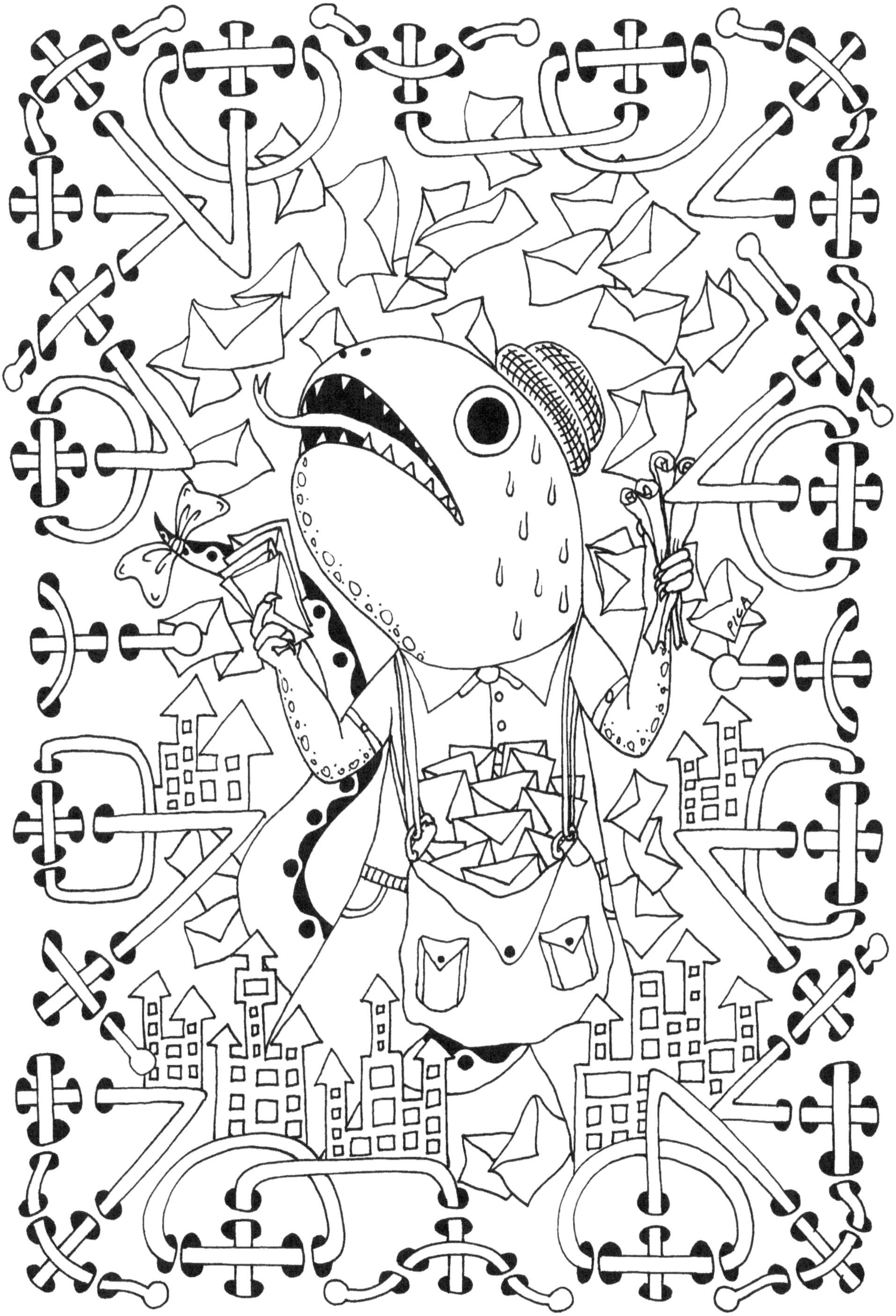
PICA

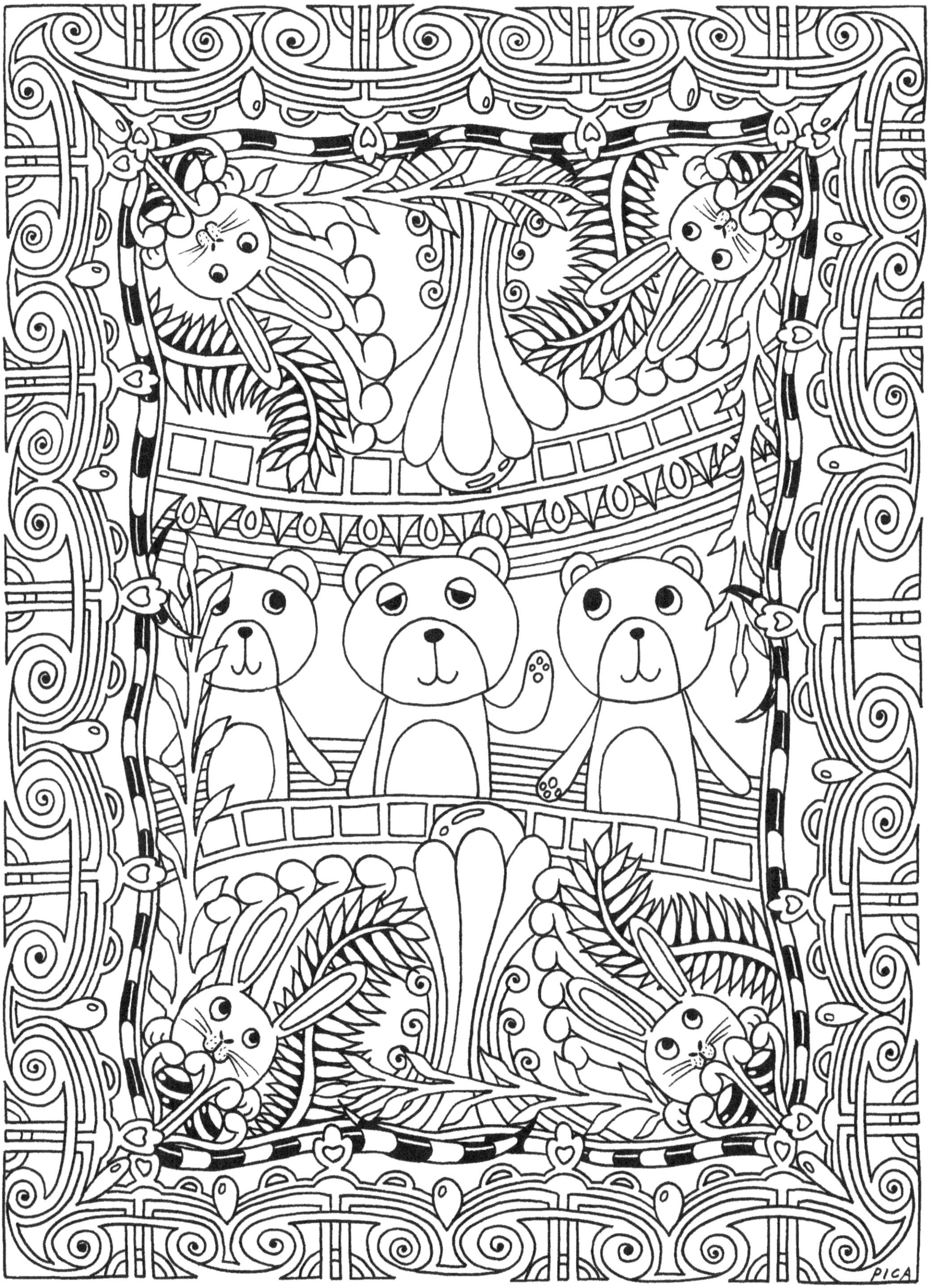
PICA

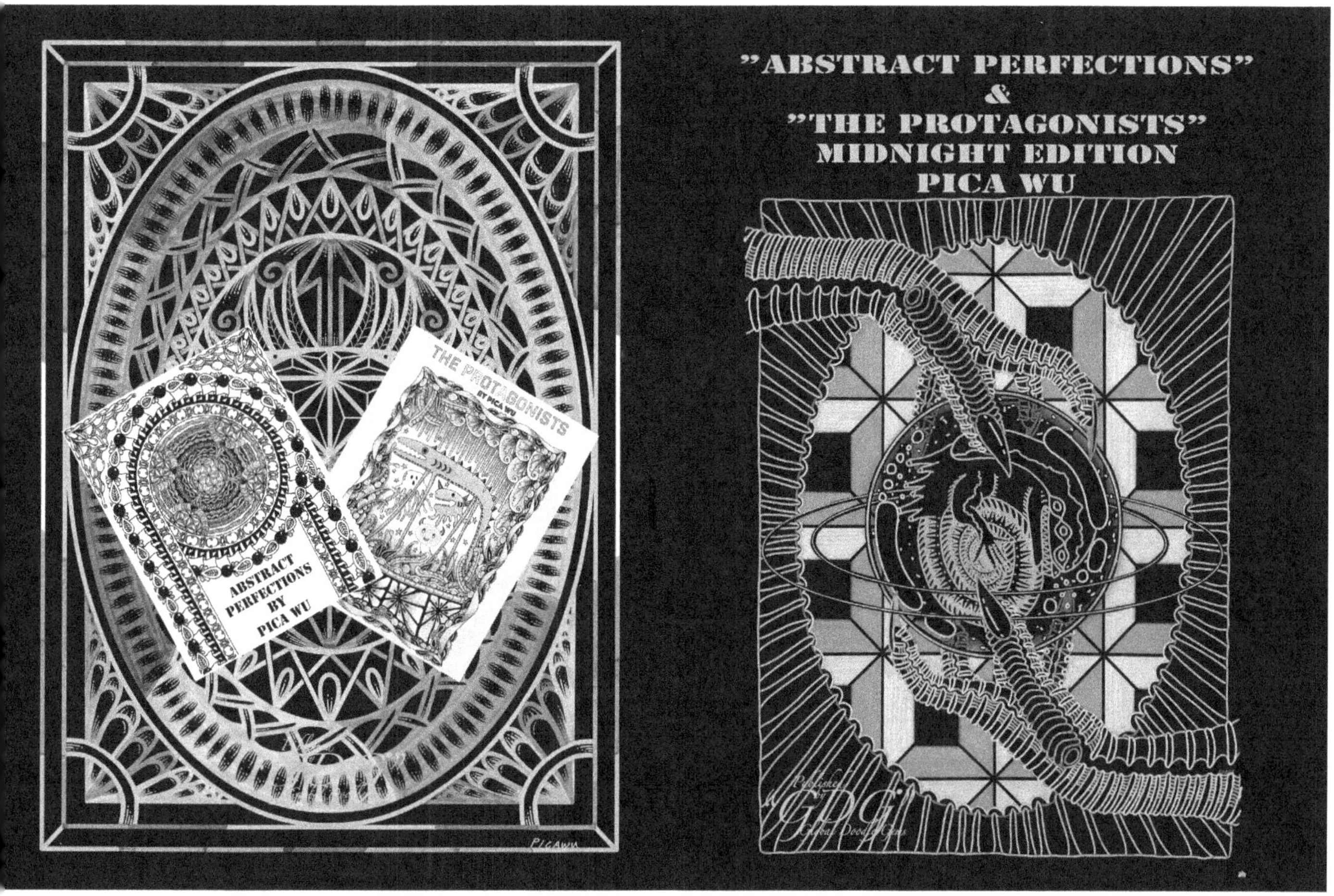

CHECK OUT THE MIDNIGHT EDITION THAT INCLUDES BOTH THE FIRST BOOK "ABSTRACT PERFECTIONS" AND "THE PROTAGONISTS"

SEE INSIDE ON THE FOLLOWING PAGES

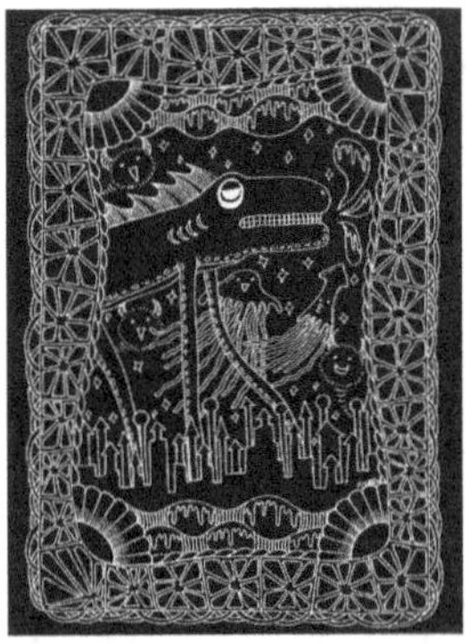
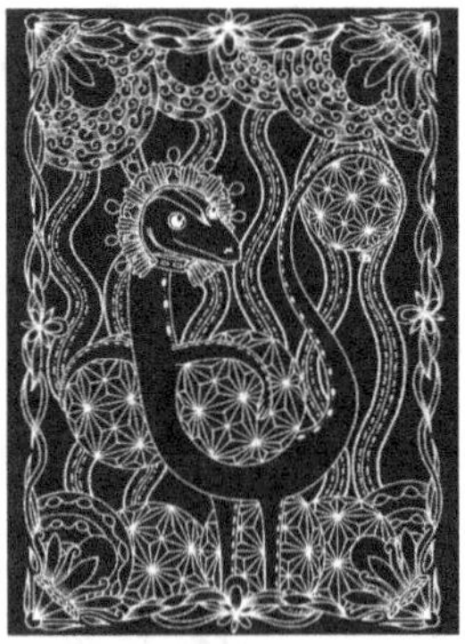
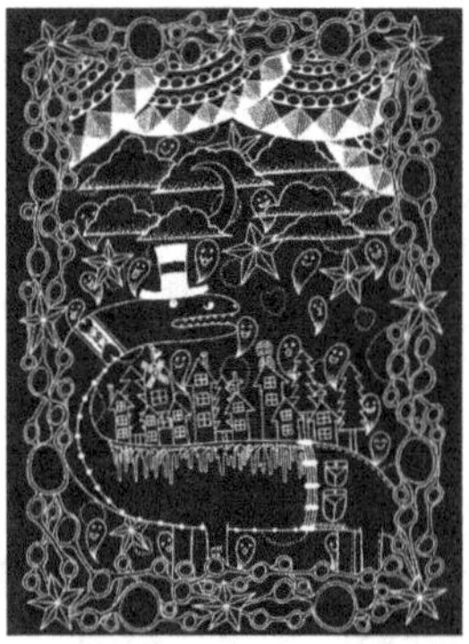
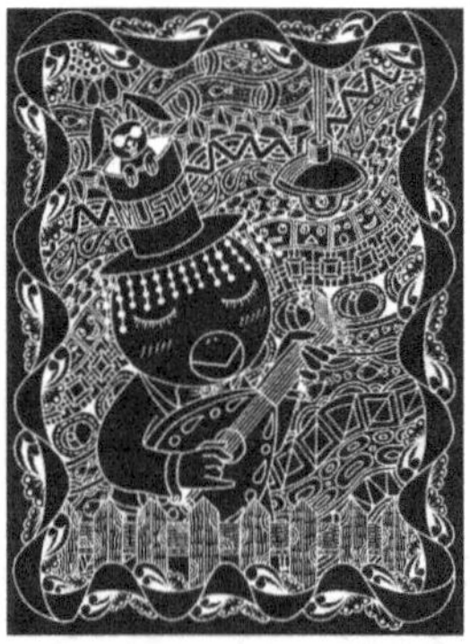
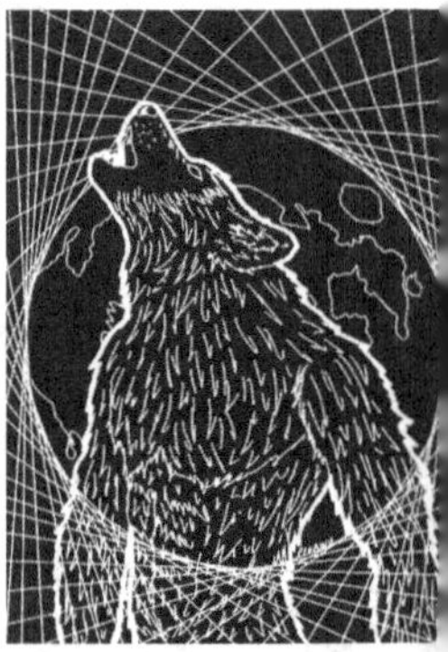
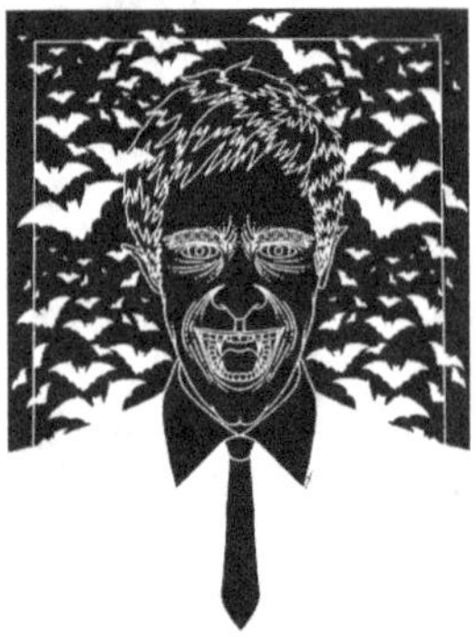
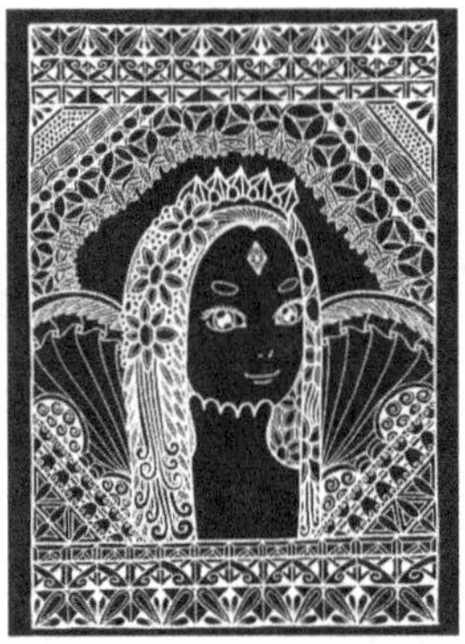
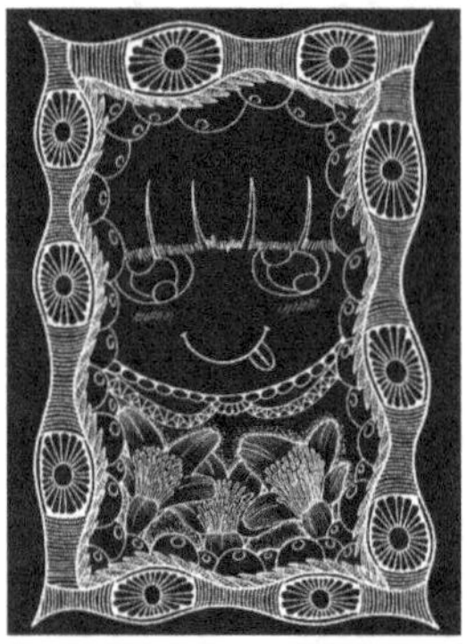
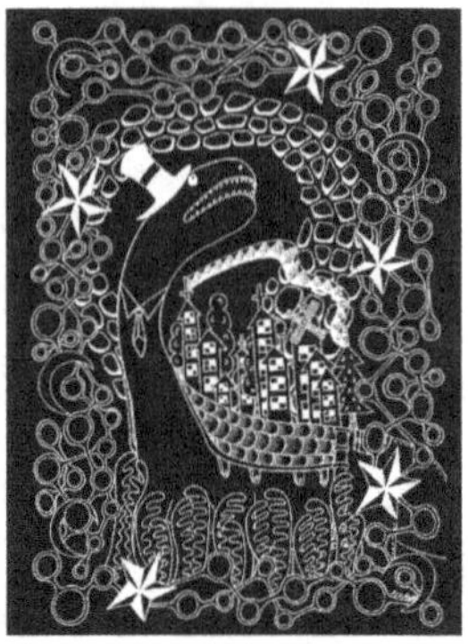
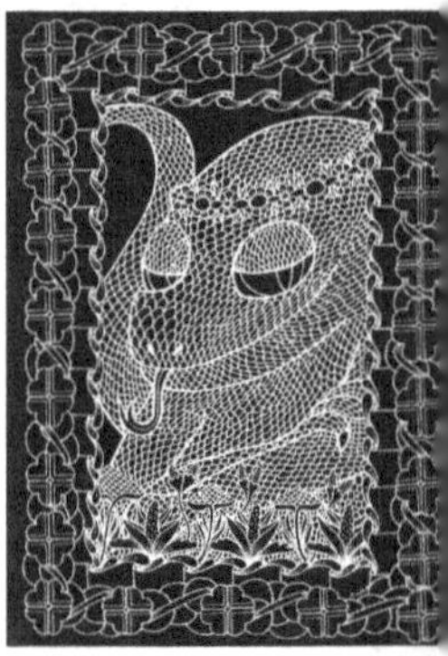
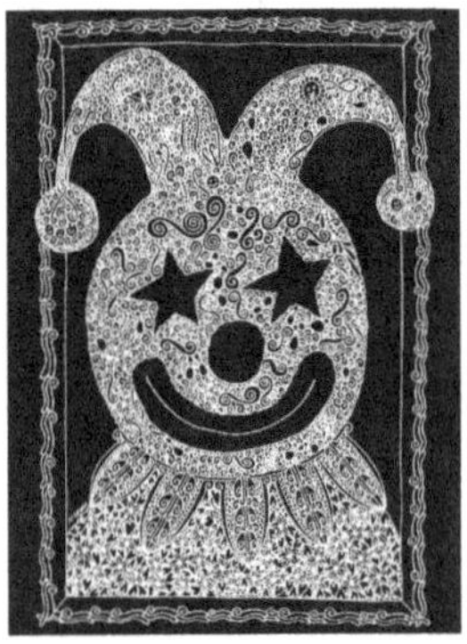
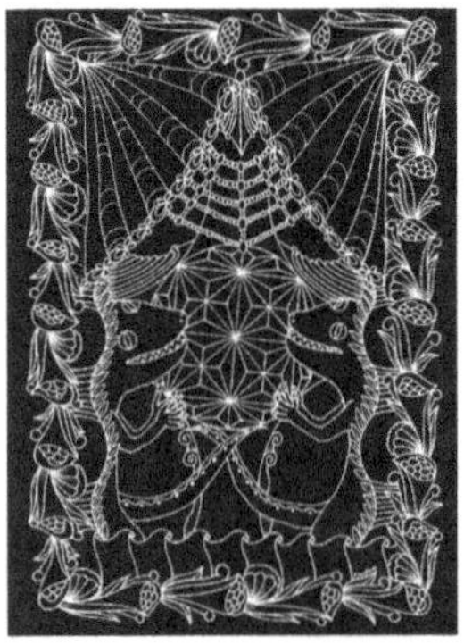
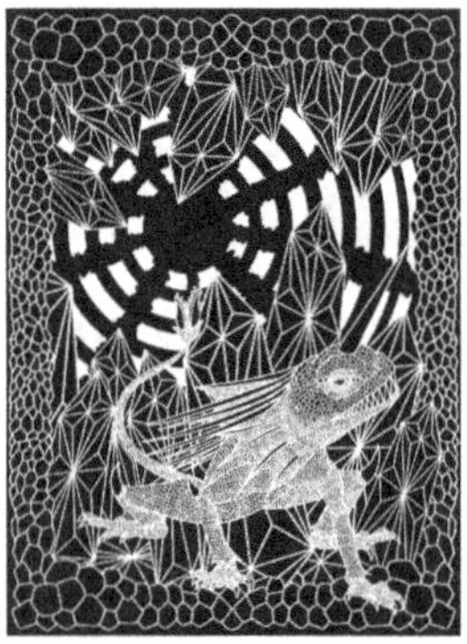
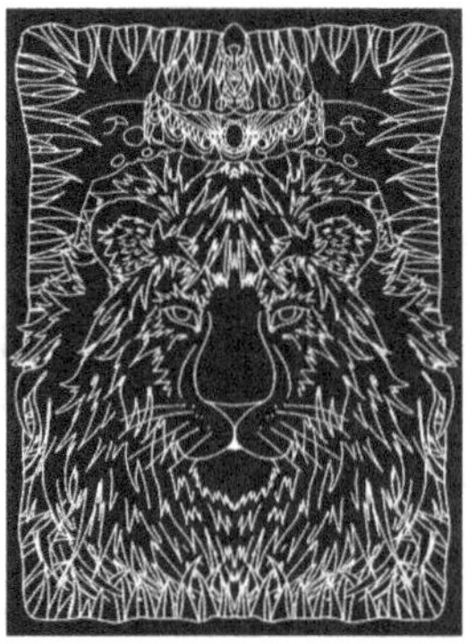
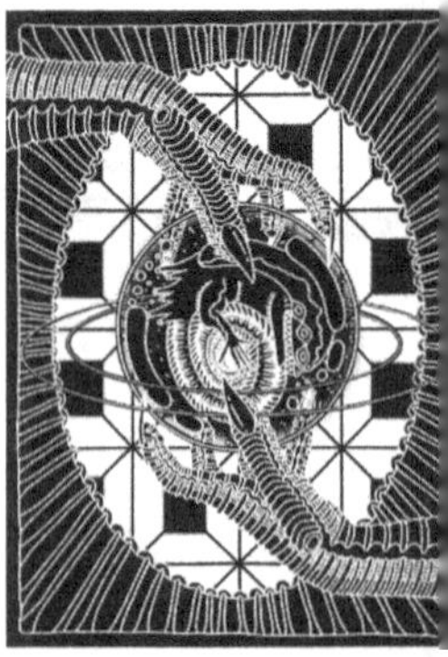
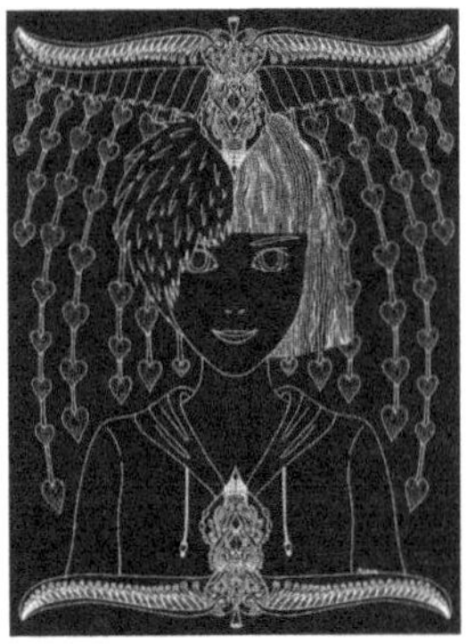
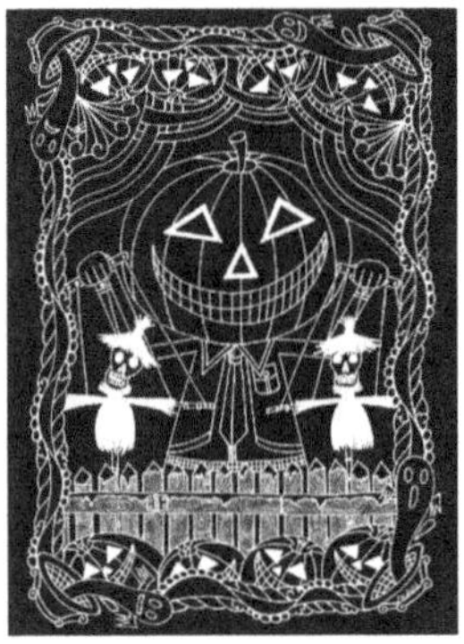
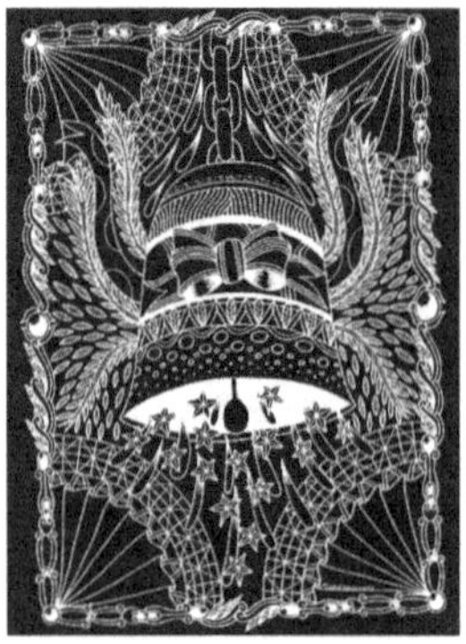
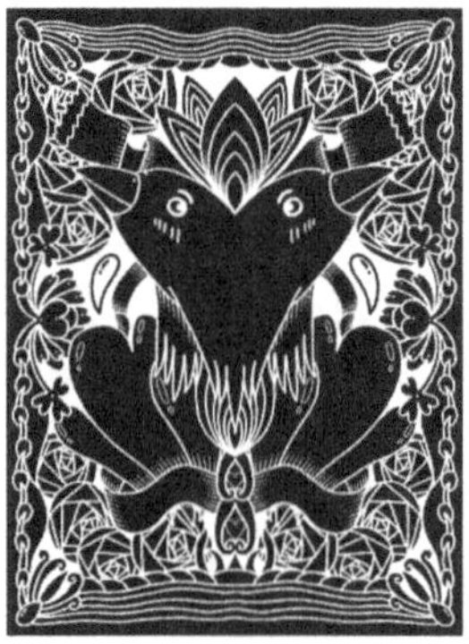
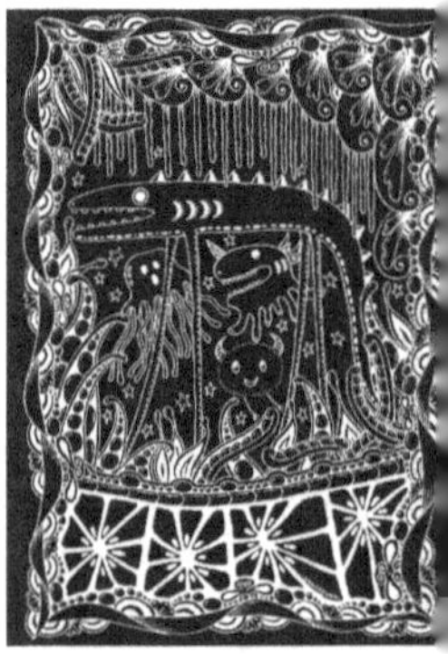
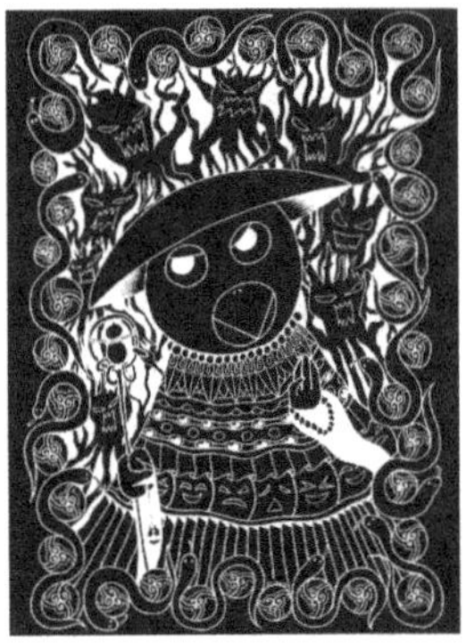
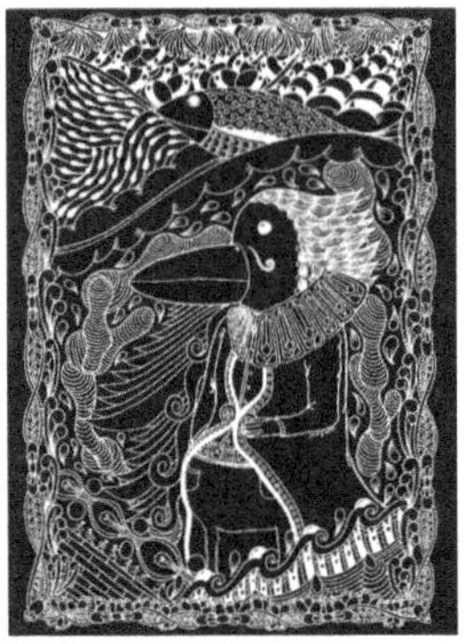
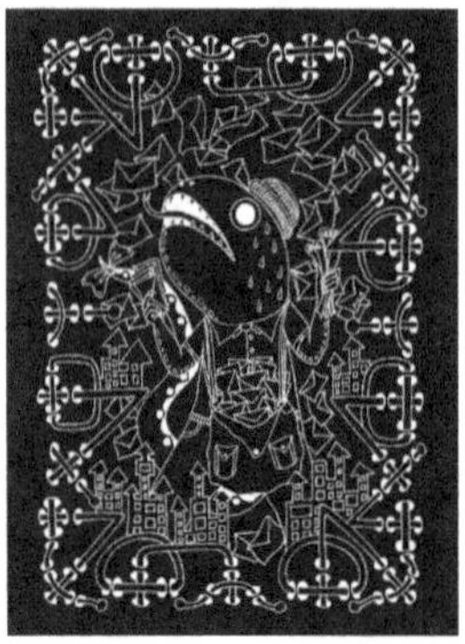
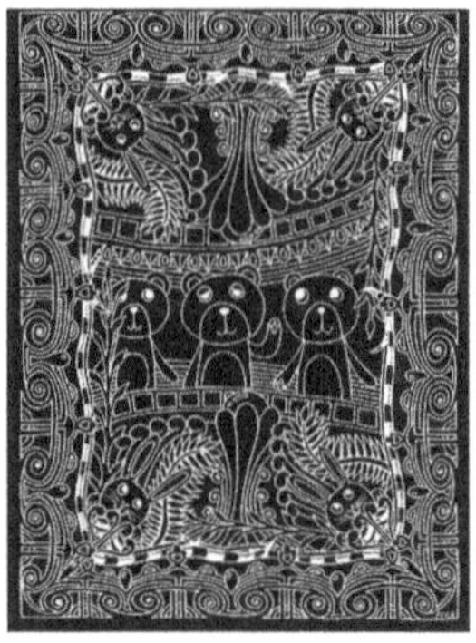
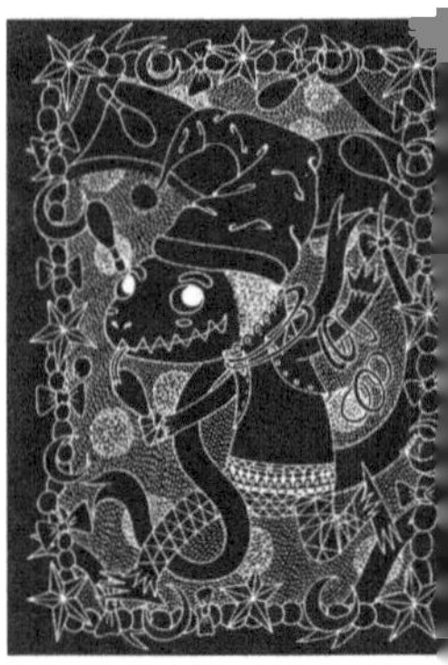

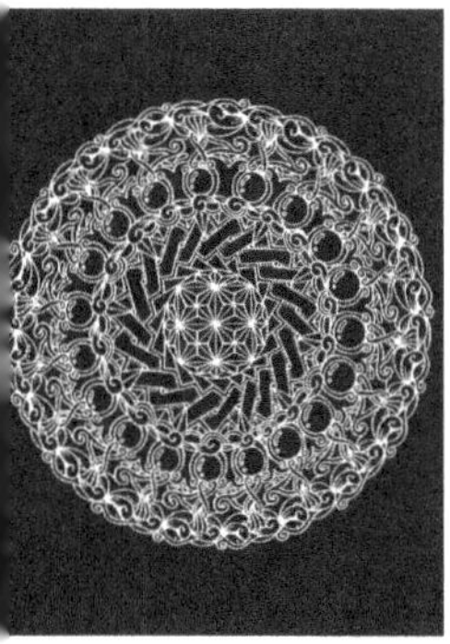
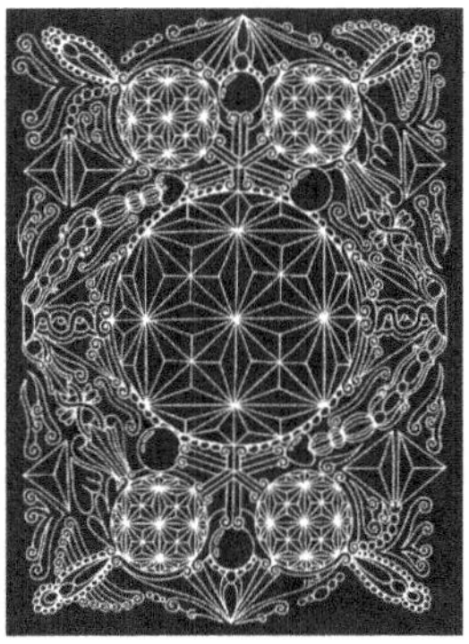
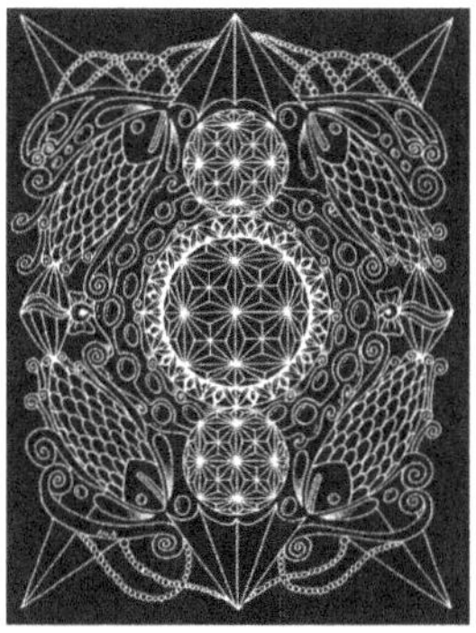
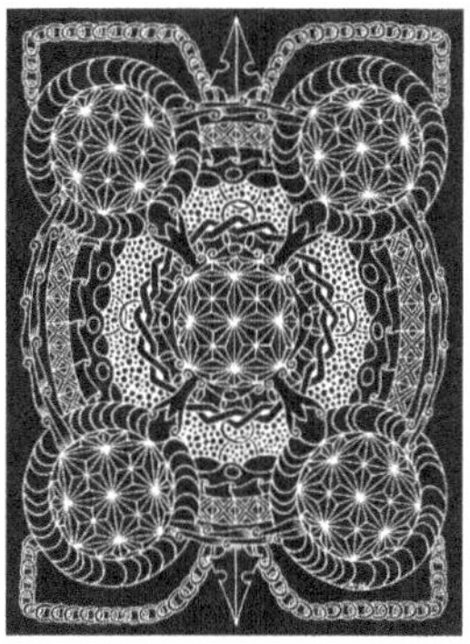
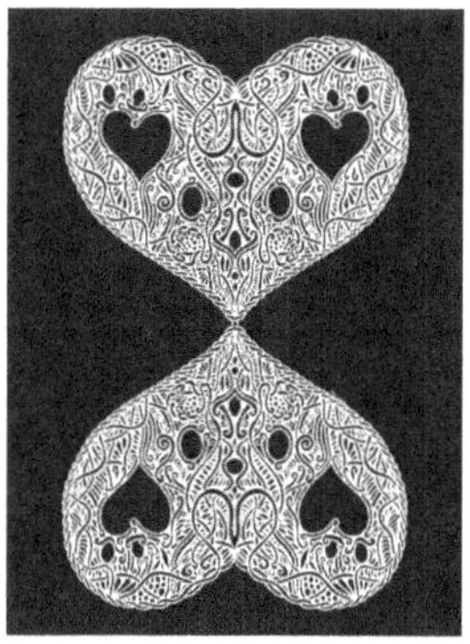
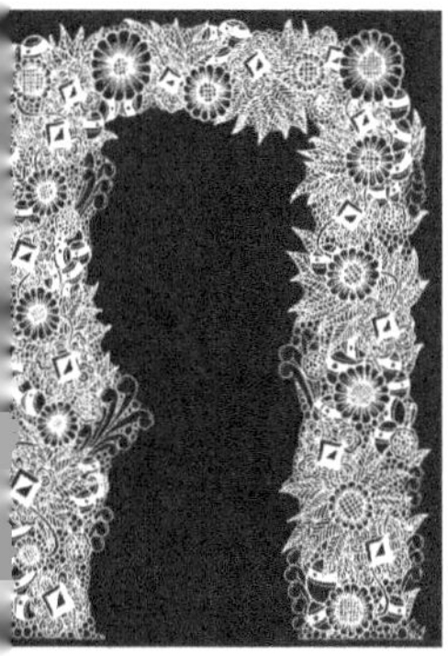
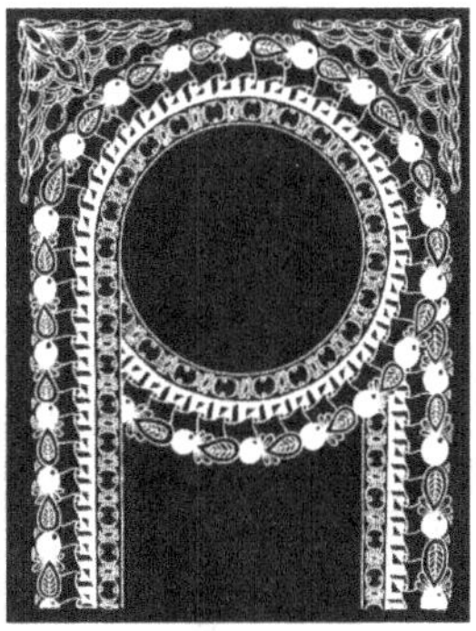
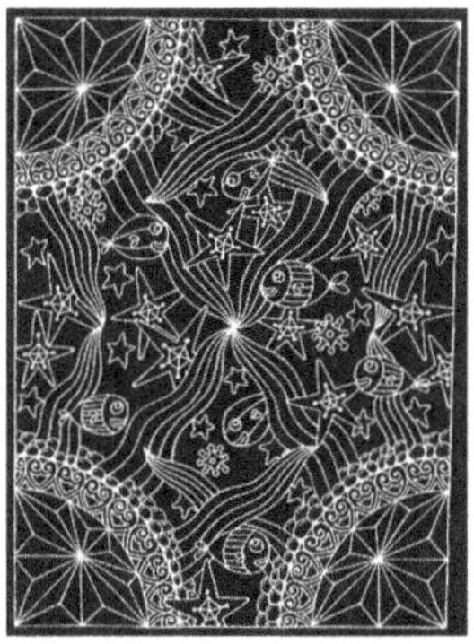
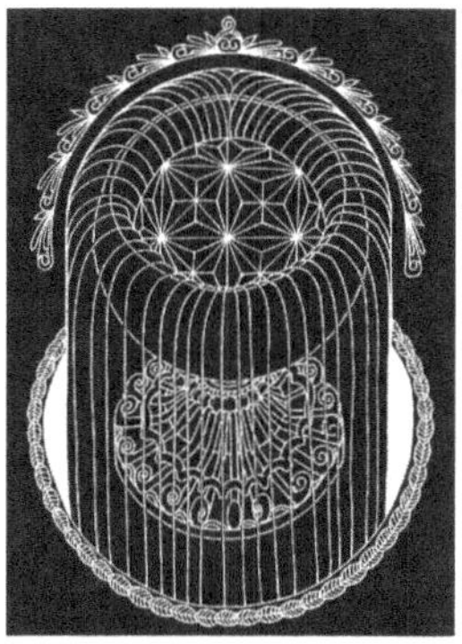
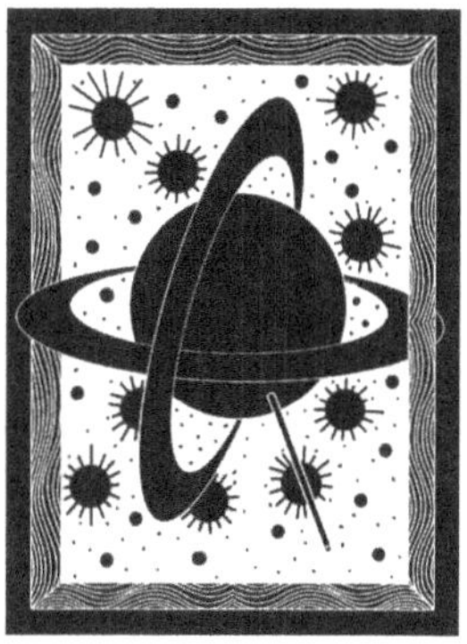
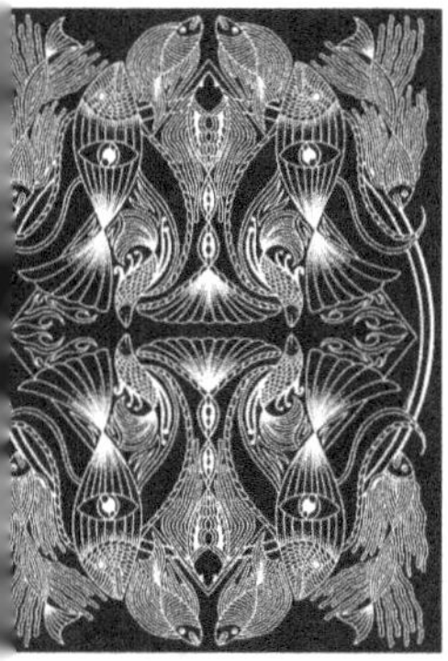
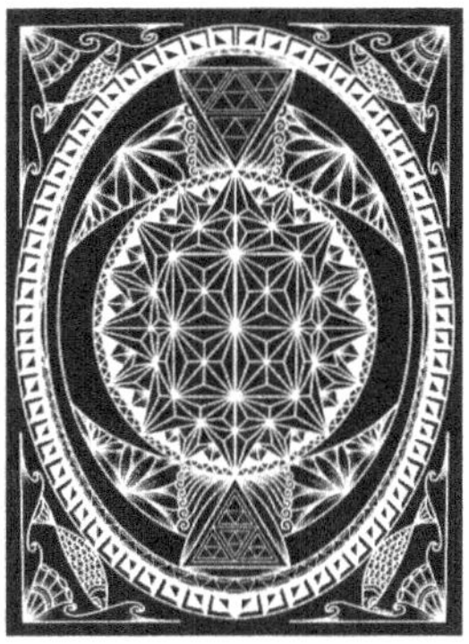
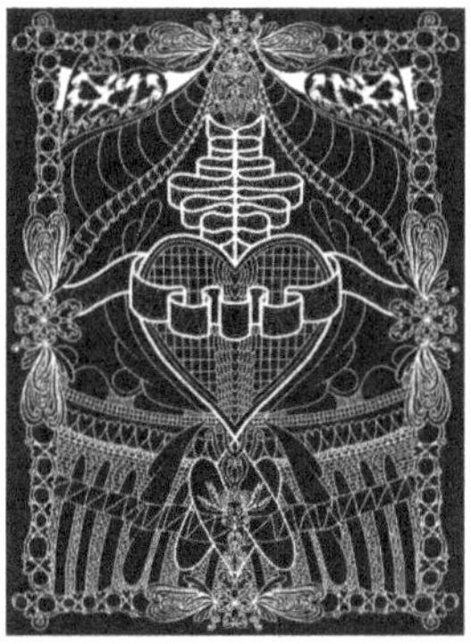
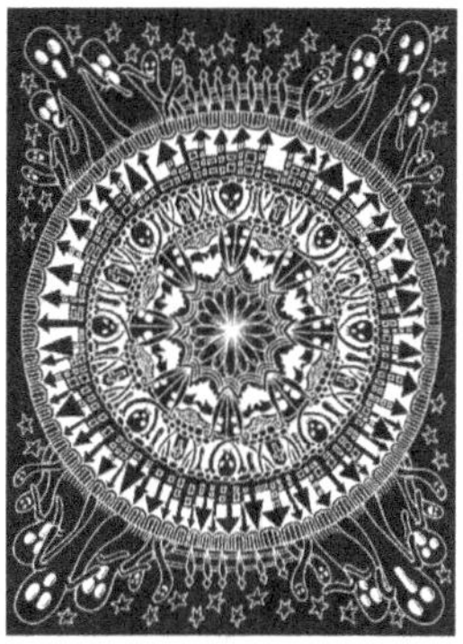
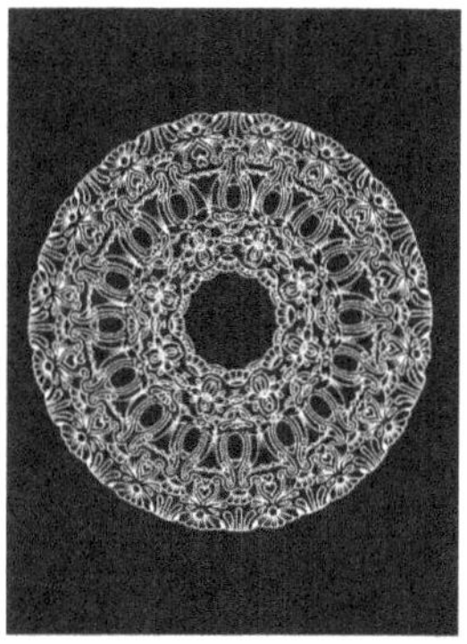
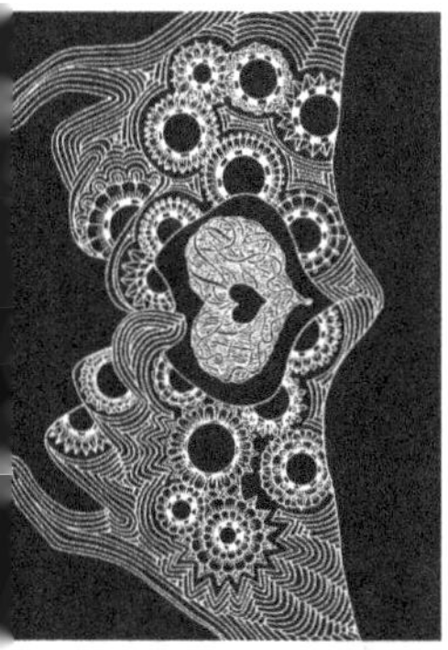
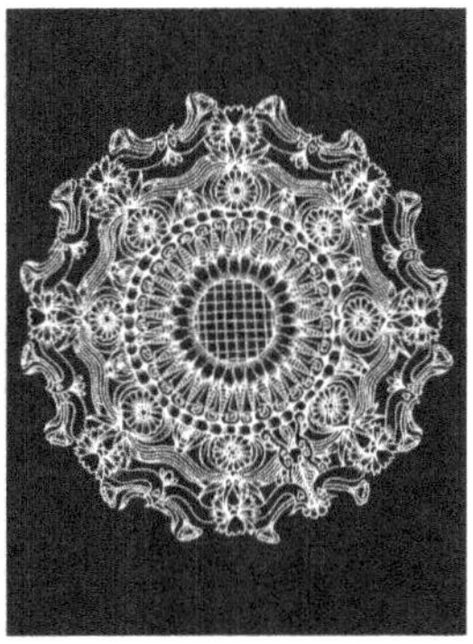
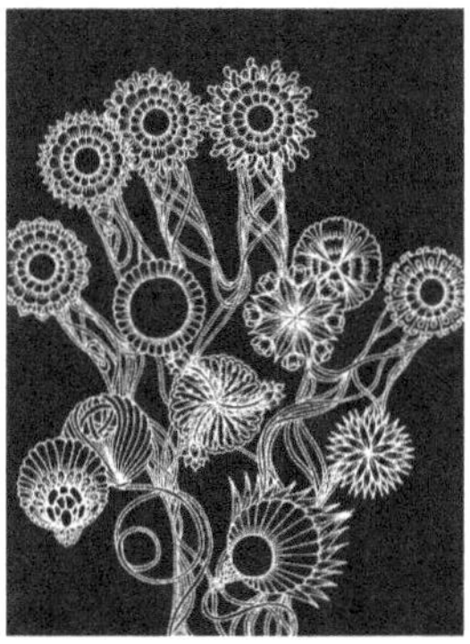
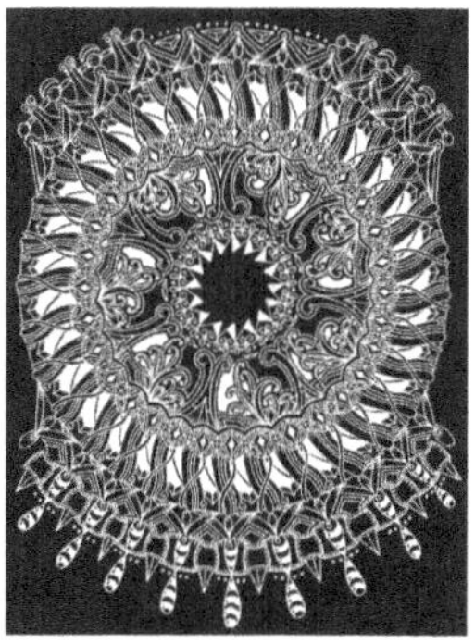
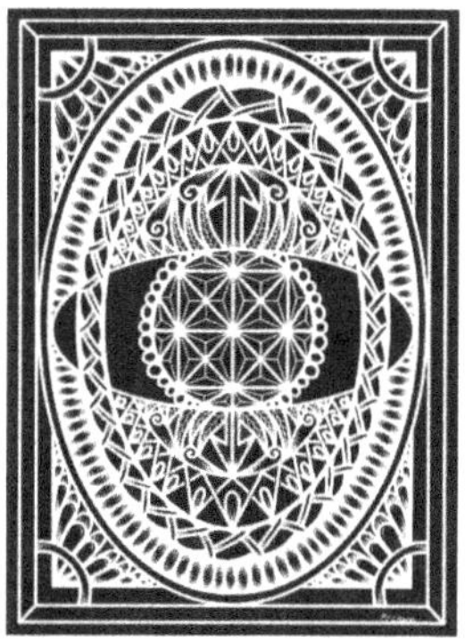
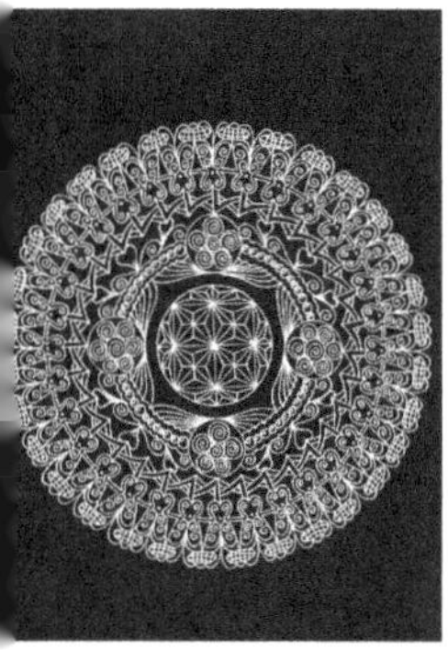
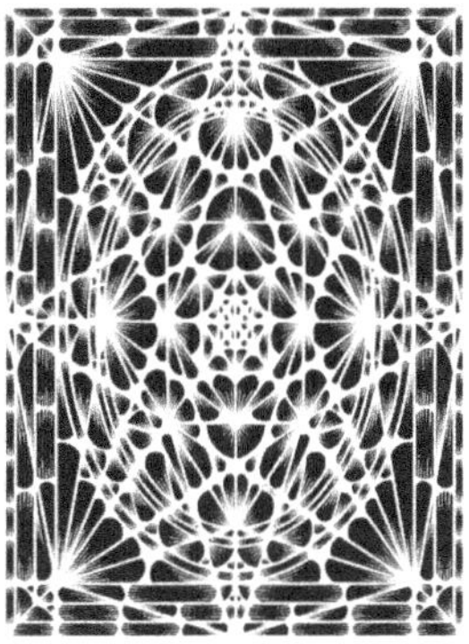
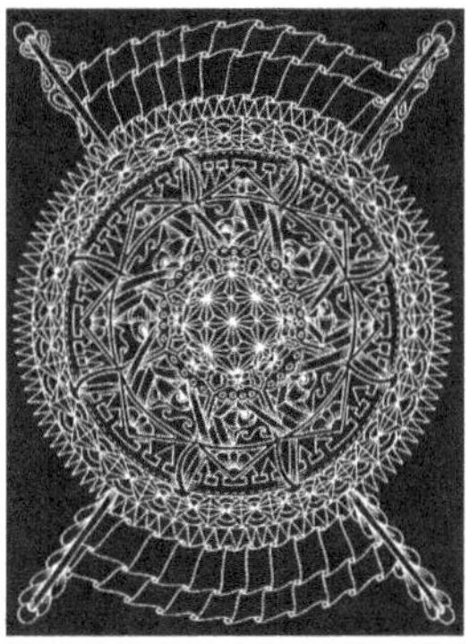
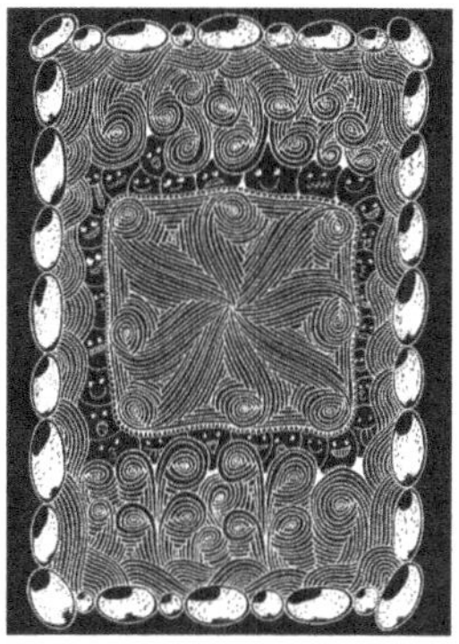
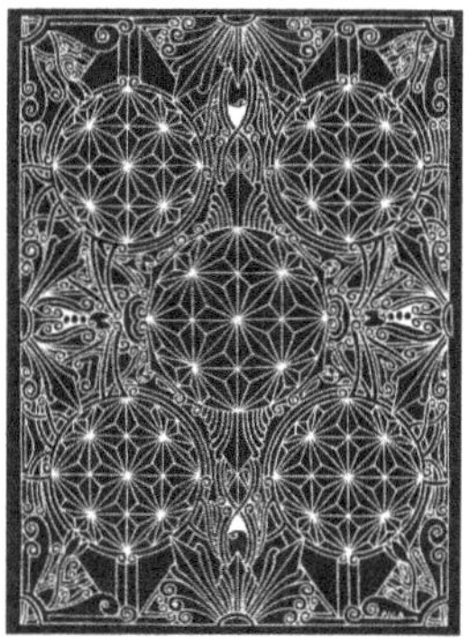

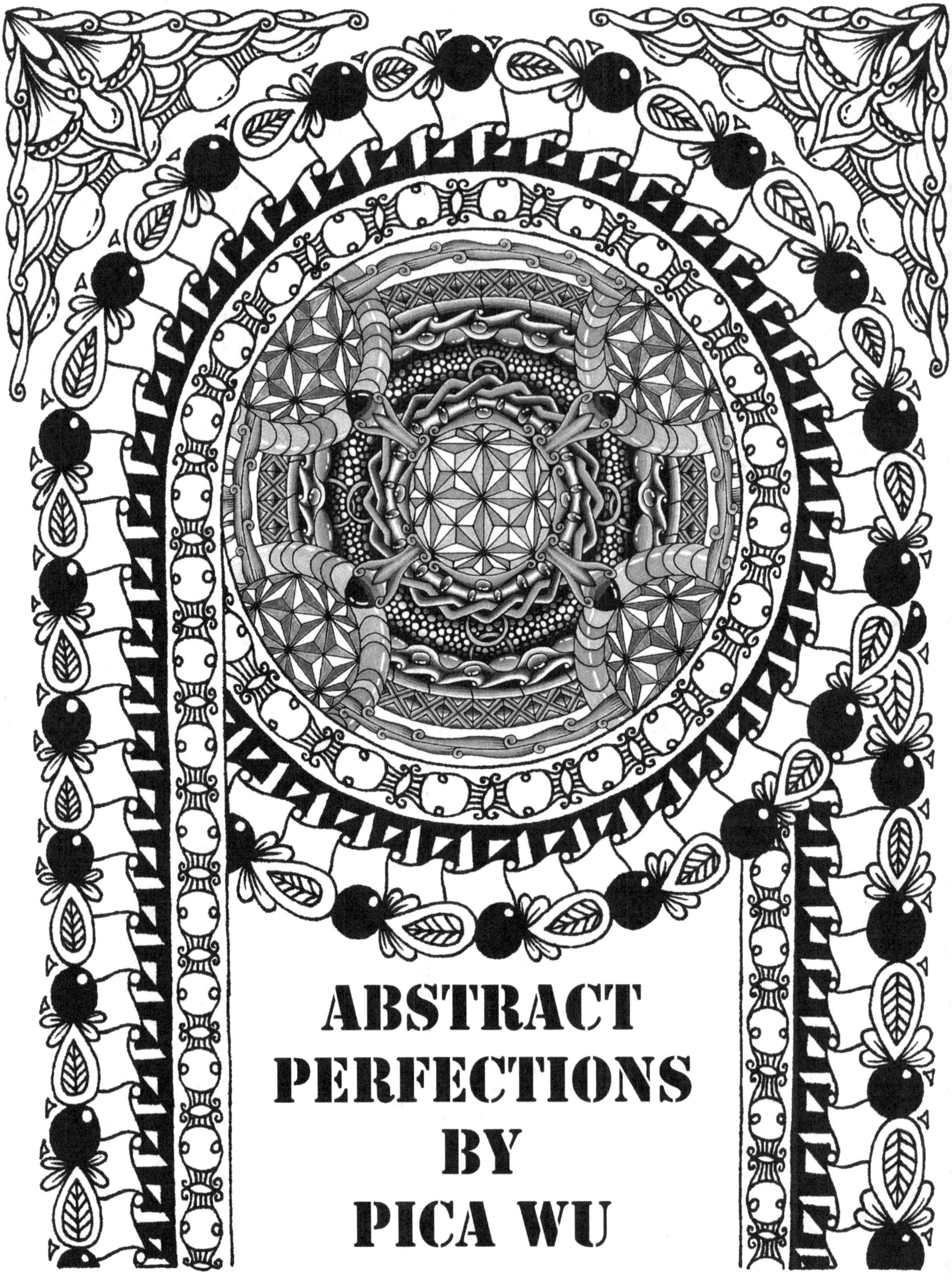
ABSTRACT
PERFECTIONS
BY
PICA WU

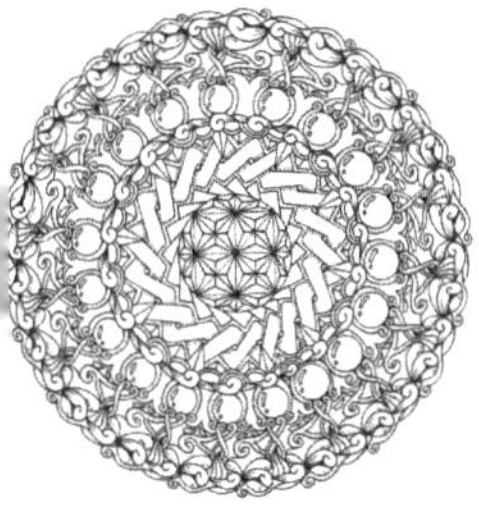
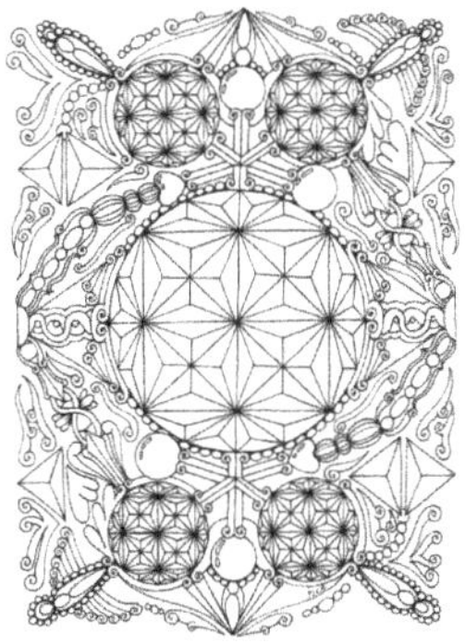
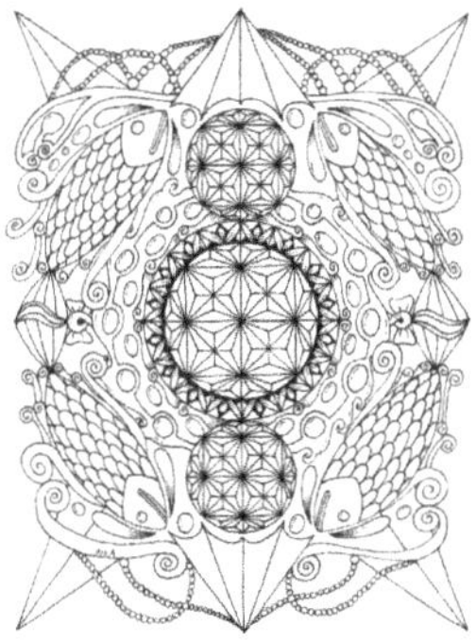
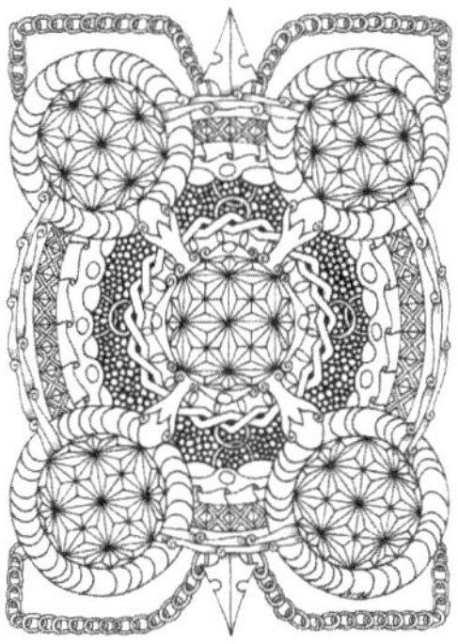
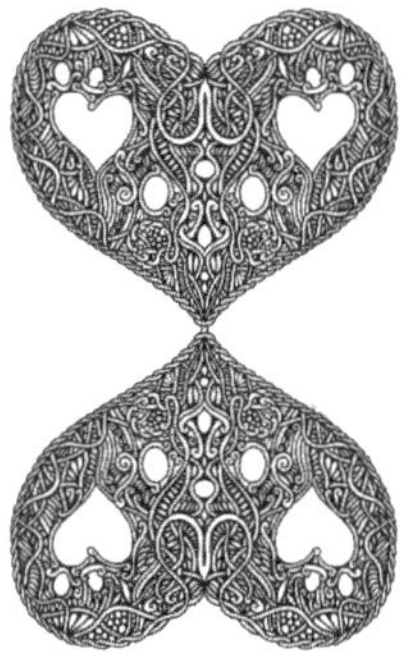
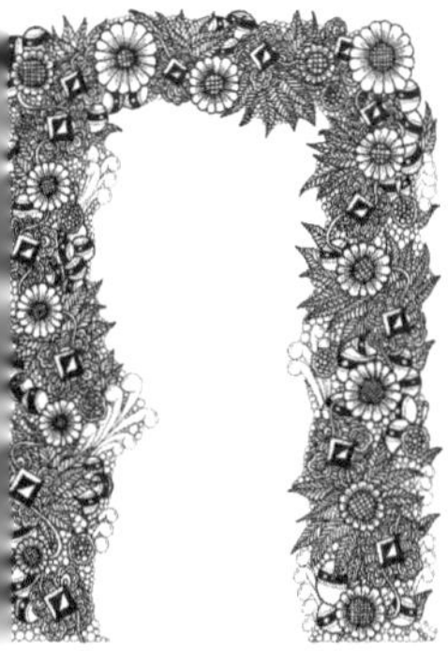
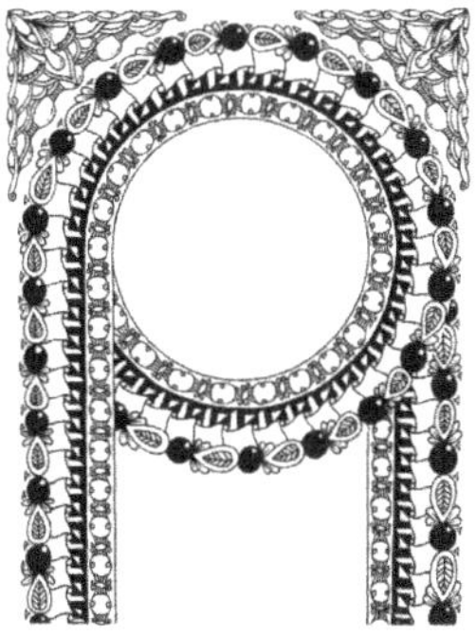
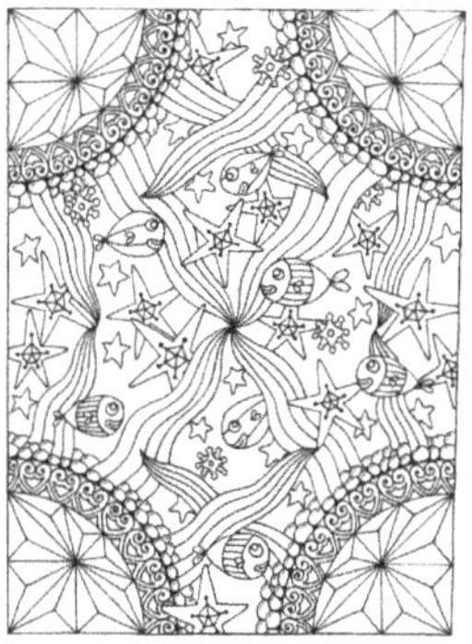
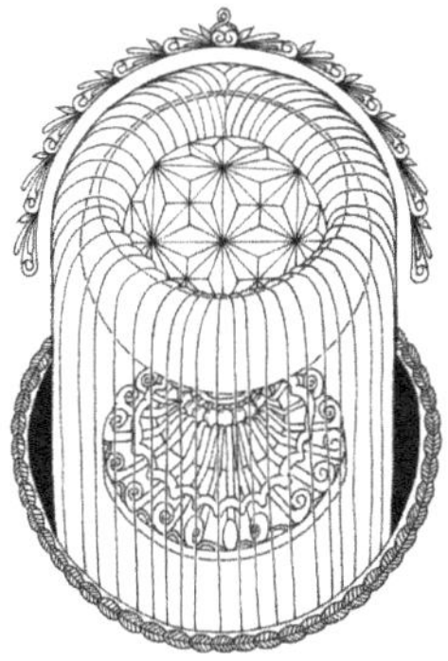
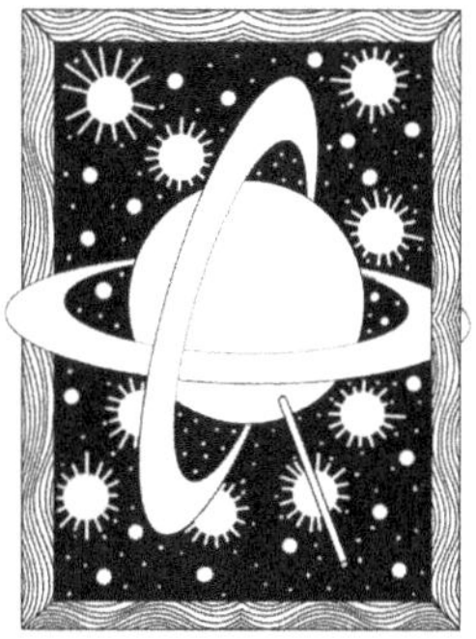
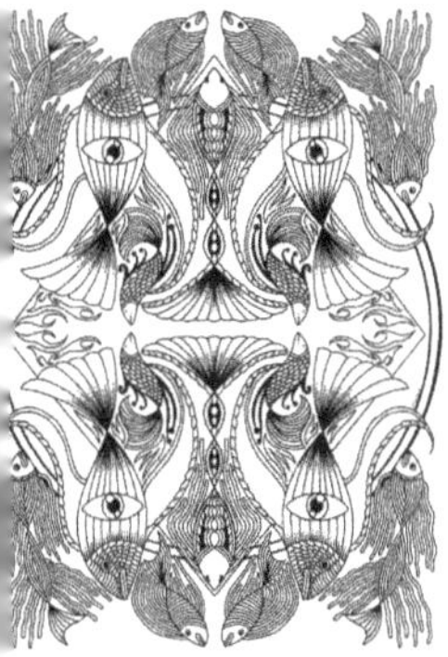
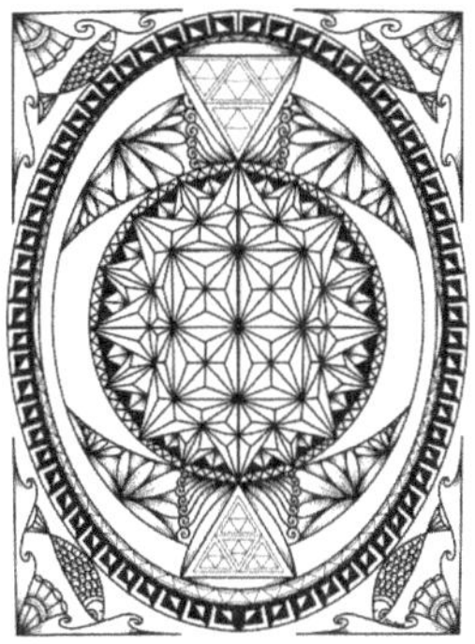
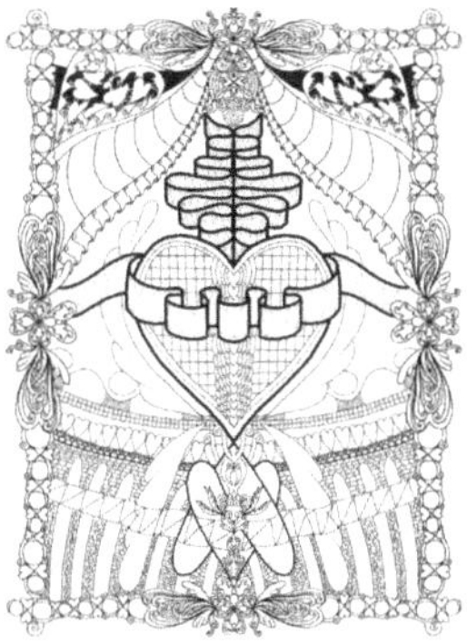
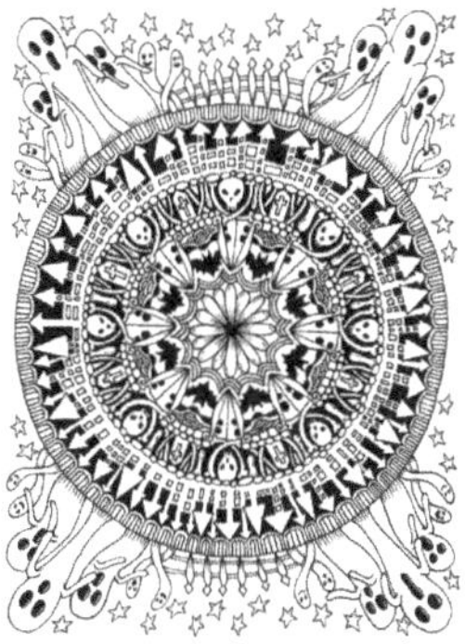
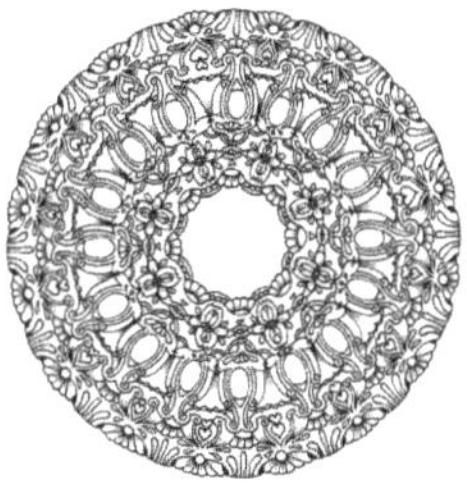
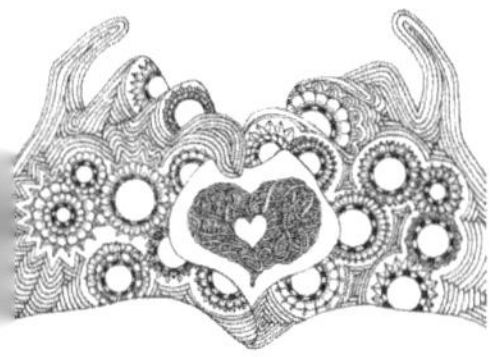
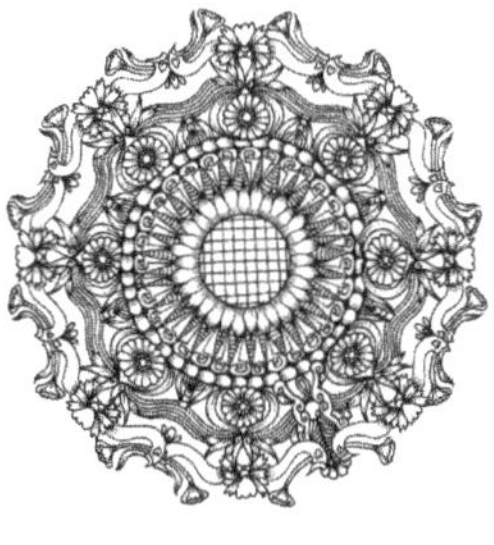
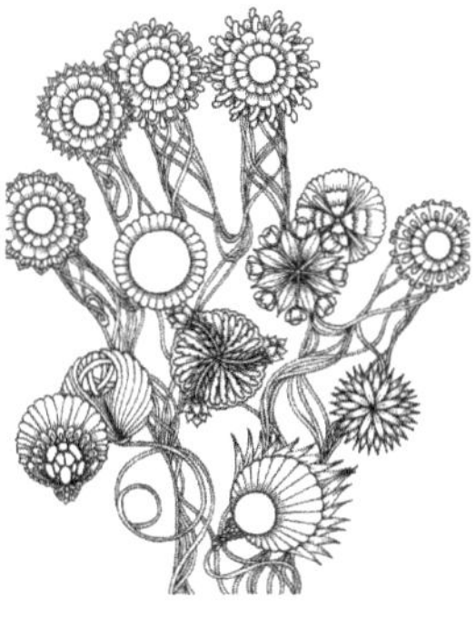
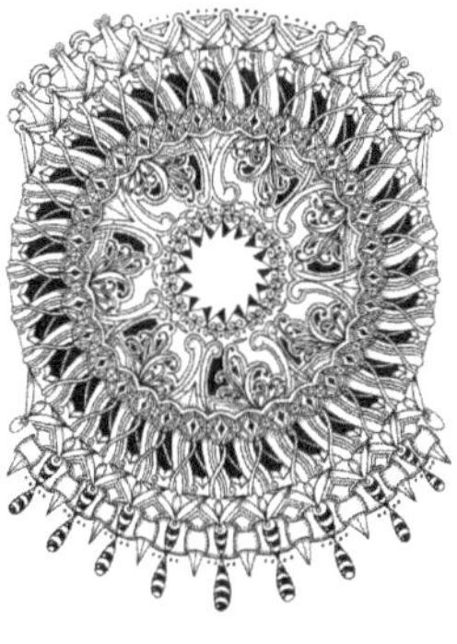
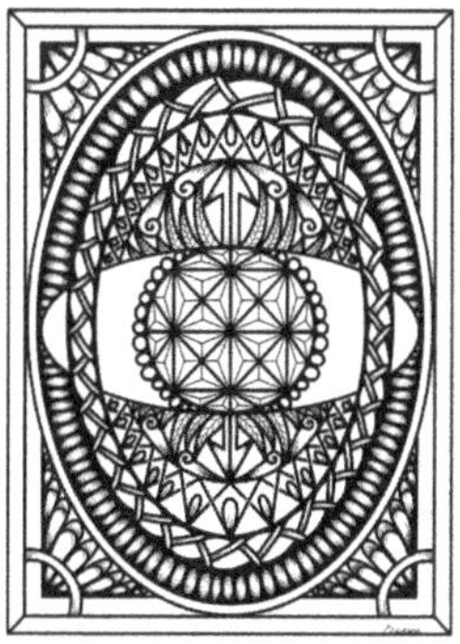
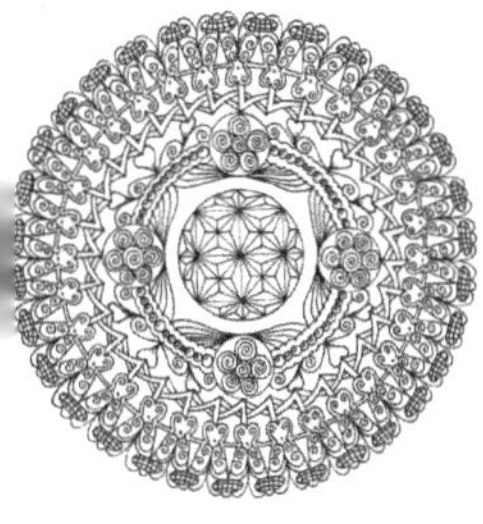
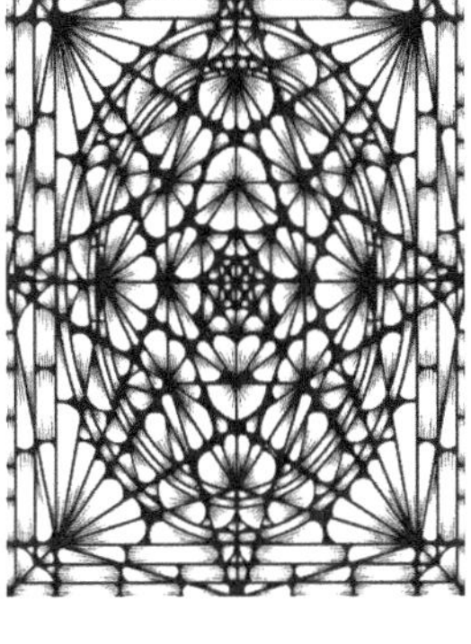
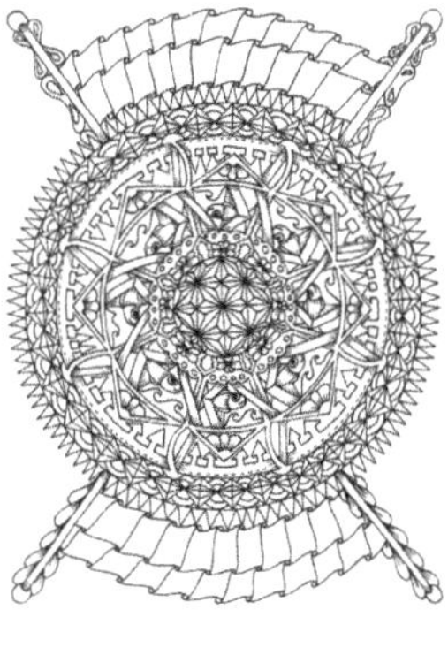
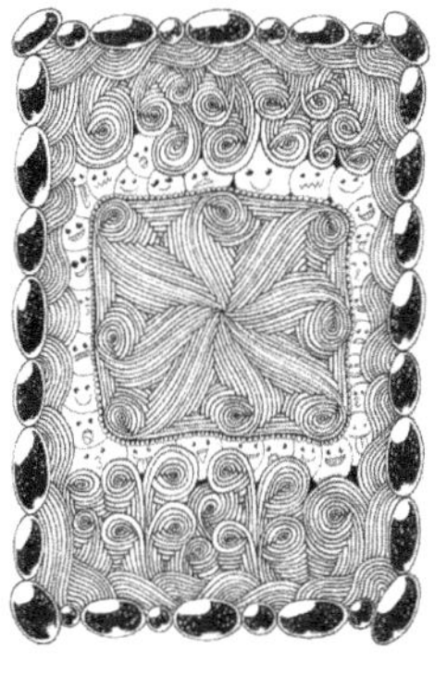
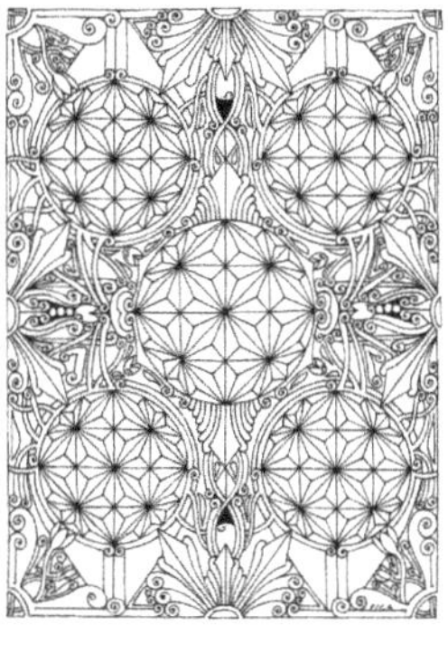

Test your colors here on the samples from
"My Pocket Coloring Companion"
&
"My Coloring Companion"

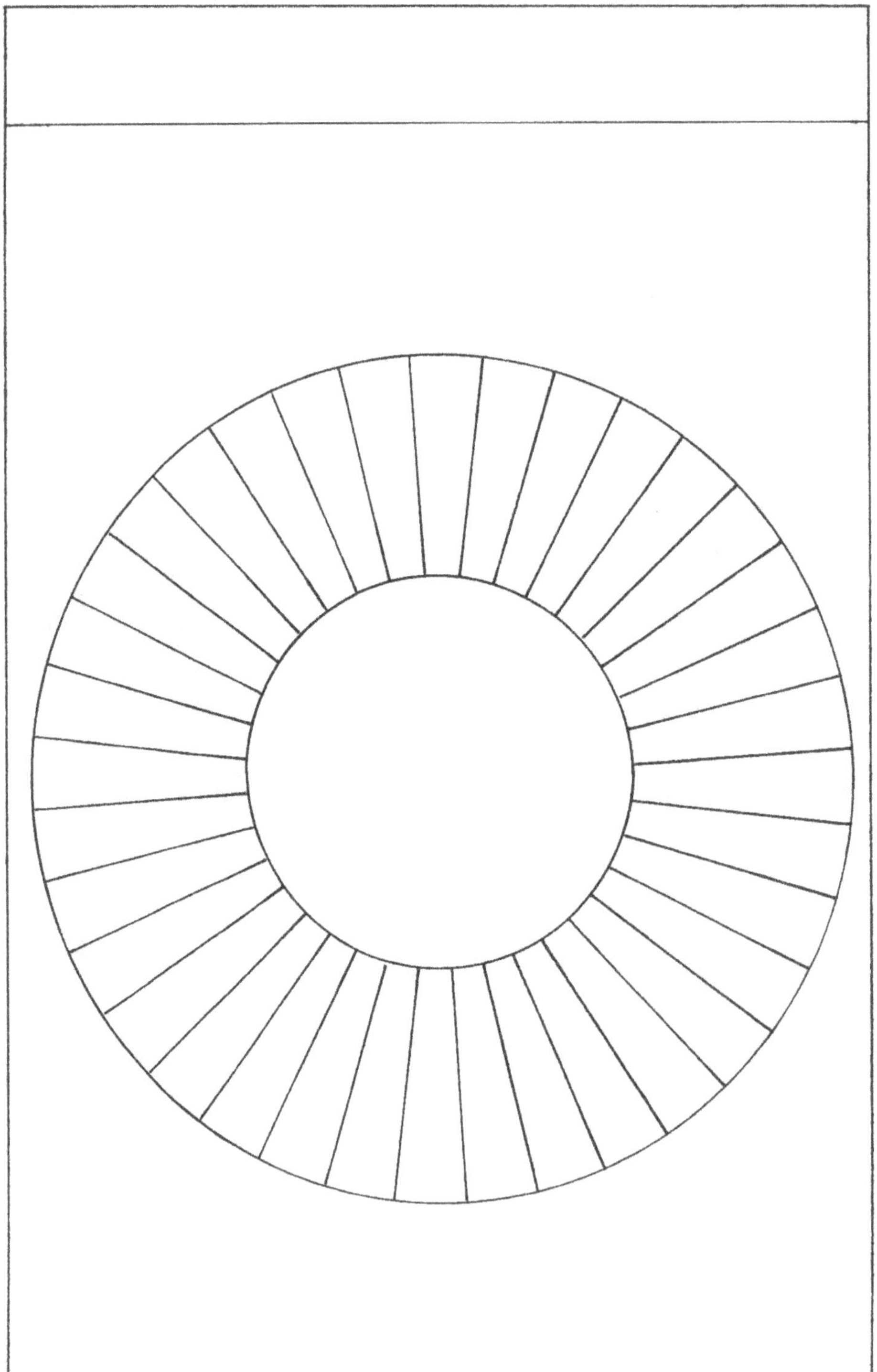

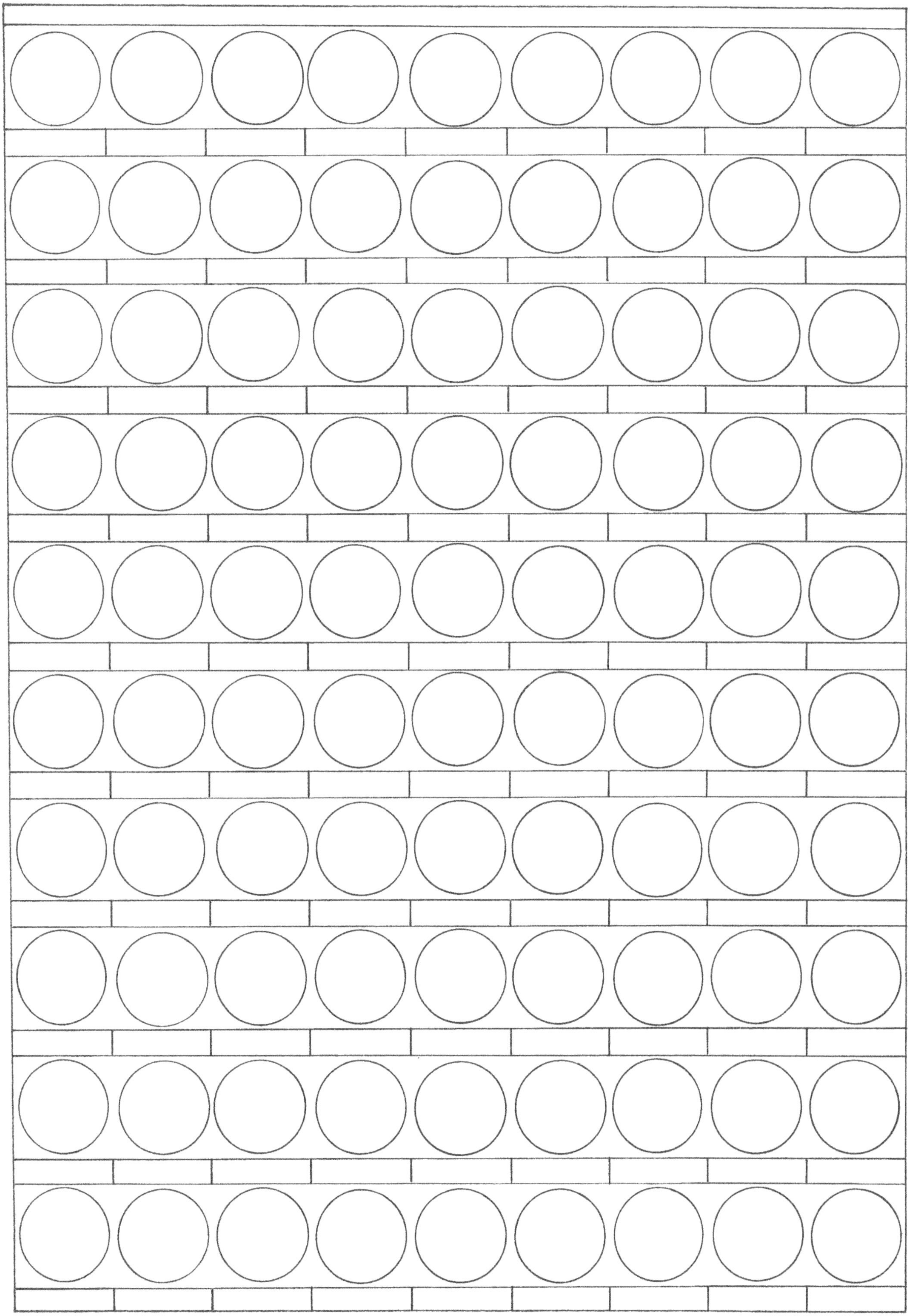

www.ingramcontent.com/pod-product-compliance
Lightning Source LLC
Chambersburg PA
CBHW080002230526
45470CB00008B/2835
* 9 7 8 8 7 7 2 0 1 0 0 2 1 *